RAND M^cNALLY

Atlas

of Western Civilization

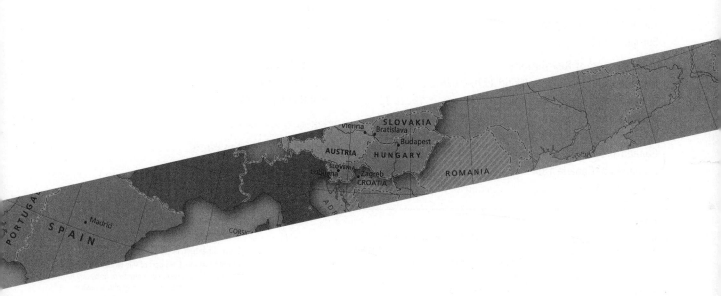

 HOUGHTON MIFFLIN

Table of Contents

Credits

Cartography and Research
Robert K. Argersinger
Gregory Babiak
Barbara Strassheim Benstead
Justin Griffin
Susan Hudson
Felix Lopez
David Simmons
Andrew Skinner
Raymond Tobiaski
Howard Veregin

Editor
Brett R. Gover

Contributing Editors and Consultants
Janet Abu-Lughod, New School of Social Research
Guy Allito, University of Chicago
Ralph Austen, University of Chicago
George Grantham, Social Studies Liaison
Alan Kolata, University of Chicago
James F. Marran, Chairman Emeritus, Social Studies, New Trier High School
David Northrup, Boston College
R. R. Palmer, Princeton University
John Ruedy, Georgetown University
John Woods, University of Chicago

Design
Rand McNally Design

Cover Photos
Copyright ©Getty/royalty free

Copyright ©2006 by Rand McNally & Company
All rights reserved. No part of this work may be reproduced or transmitted in any form or by any means electronic or mechanical, including photocopying and recording, or by information storage or retrieval system, except by permission of the publisher.

Printed in the United States of America

Rand McNally & Company
Skokie, Illinois 60076

10 9 8 7 6 5 4 3 2

ISBN: 0-618-84194-6

Introduction

Information about the past is compiled, stored, and made accessible in a variety of ways. One of these ways is historical maps. Historical maps provide a chronology of important events and show the impact these events had on the places where they occurred. Historical maps support and extend information from primary historical resources such as letters, treaties, and census data. Historical maps are summaries of past events in graphic form.

The maps in the Rand McNally *Atlas of Western Civilization* portray the rich panoply of this civilization from its origins in Mesopotamia and the Nile Valley in the third millennium B.C. through the beginning of the 21st century. They show how cultures were linked and how they interacted. The maps make it clear that history is not static. Rather, it is about change and movement across time. The maps show change by presenting the dynamics of expansion, cooperation, and conflict.

Benefits of Using the Rand McNally *Atlas of Western Civilization*

Events gain fuller meaning.

Knowing where events took place gives them fuller meaning and often explains causes and effects. For example, the map showing Russia's expansion in Europe clearly illustrates that a major goal of the czars was to access warm-water ports that would connect their realm to the world's seas and oceans.

Connections among events are clarified.

Through the visual power of historical maps, the links between and among events become clearer. The maps showing diffusion of languages and religions are good illustrations of this.

Similarities and differences become apparent.

The maps in this historical atlas provide the opportunity to compare and contrast places over time. For example, the series of Roman Empire maps present snapshots of the empire at three different points in time.

The influence of sense of place is conveyed.

Maps in this atlas can convey a people's sense of place at a particular time in history. The map of Europe's Age of Discovery is a good illustration. The cartographer has deliberately centered the continent so that the map's projection reflects the extent and ambition of Europe's exploration at the end of the Renaissance.

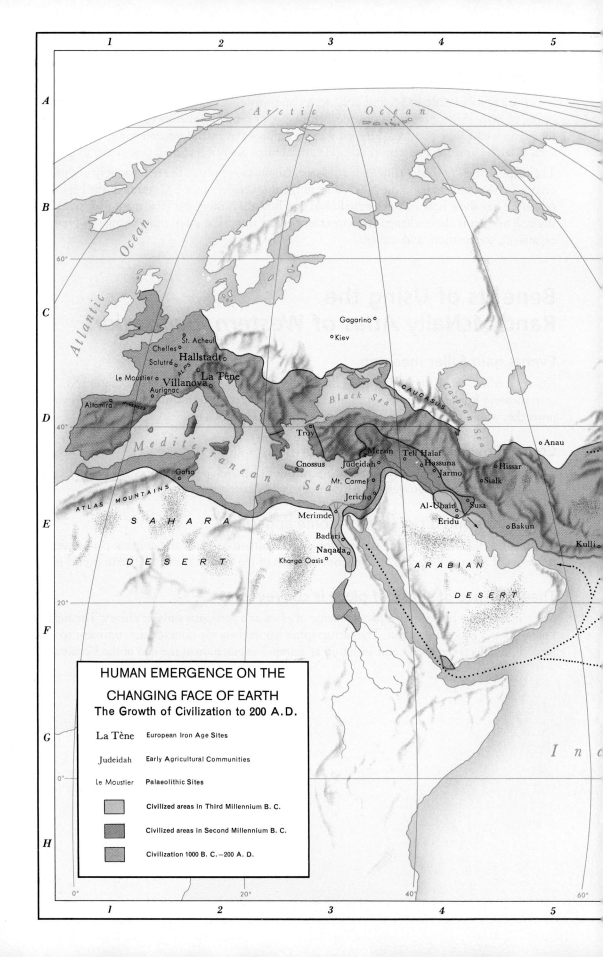

HUMAN EMERGENCE ON THE
CHANGING FACE OF EARTH
The Growth of Civilization to 200 A.D.

La Tène — European Iron Age Sites

Judeidah — Early Agricultural Communities

Le Moustier — Palaeolithic Sites

Civilized areas in Third Millennium B. C.

Civilized areas in Second Millennium B. C.

Civilization 1000 B. C.—200 A. D.

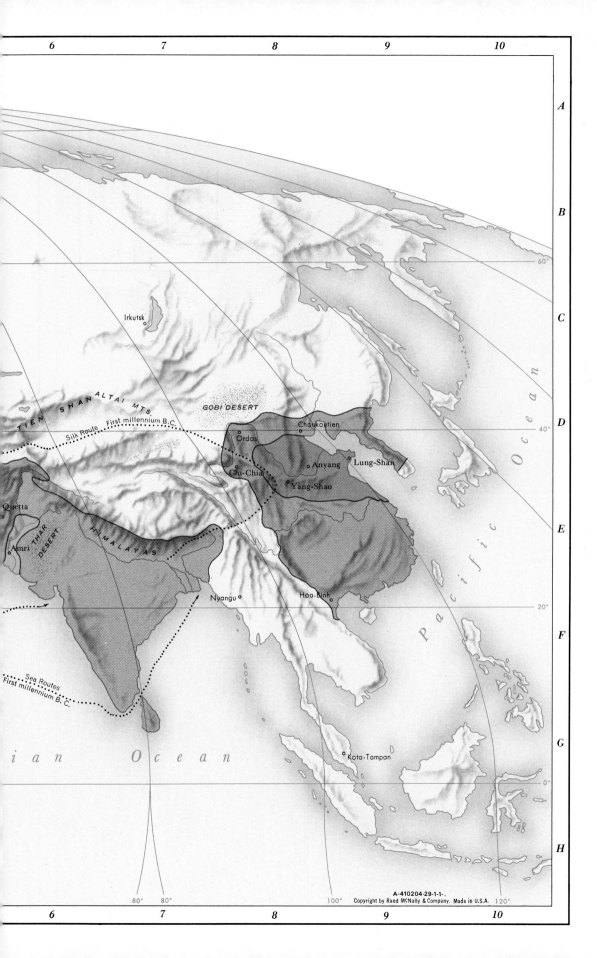

6   7   8   9   10

A

B

60°

C

Irkutsk

TIEN SHAN ALTAI MTS.
GOBI DESERT

Silk Route   First millennium B.C.
D   40°
Ordos   Choukoutien
Anyang   Lung-Shan
Chi-Chia
Yang-Shao

Quetta

THAR
Amri DESERT
HIMALAYAS
E

Nyangu   Hoa-Binh   20°
F

Sea Routes
First millennium B. C.

G

i a n   O c e a n
Kota-Tampan
0°

H

P a c i f i c   O c e a n

80°   80°   100°   120°
A-410204-29-1-1-.
Copyright by Rand McNally & Company. Made in U.S.A.

6   7   8   9   10

5

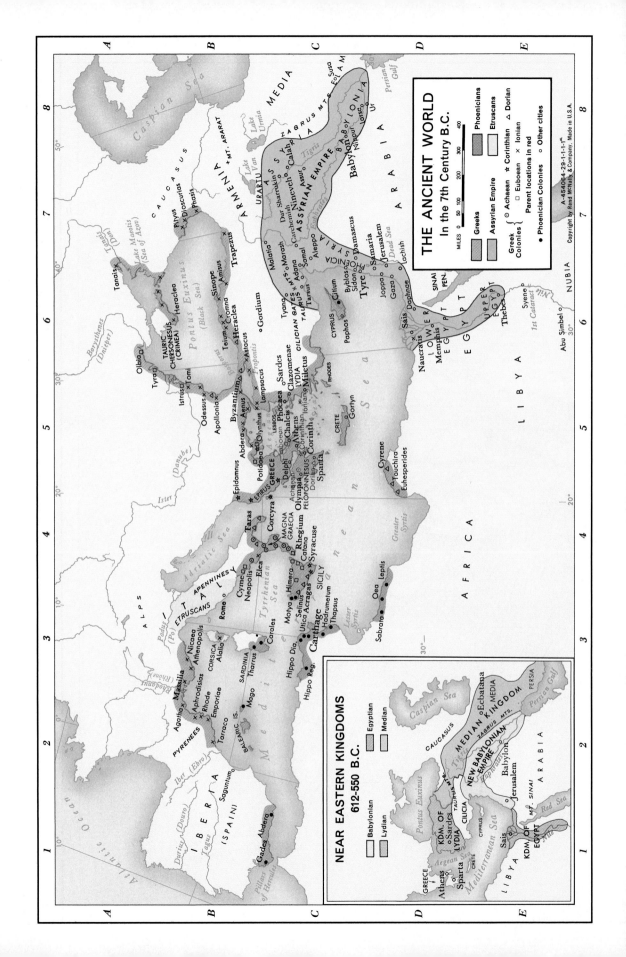

THE ANCIENT WORLD
In the 7th Century B.C.

MILES 0 50 100 200 300 400

Greeks
Assyrian Empire

Phoenicians
Etruscans

Greek Colonies:
○ Achaean   ★ Corinthian   △ Dorian
□ Euboean   × Ionian
Parent locations in red
● Phoenician Colonies   ○ Other cities

Copyright by Rand McNally & Company, Made in U.S.A.

A-454064-29-1-1-1-AL

NEAR EASTERN KINGDOMS
612-550 B.C.

Babylonian
Lydian
Egyptian
Median

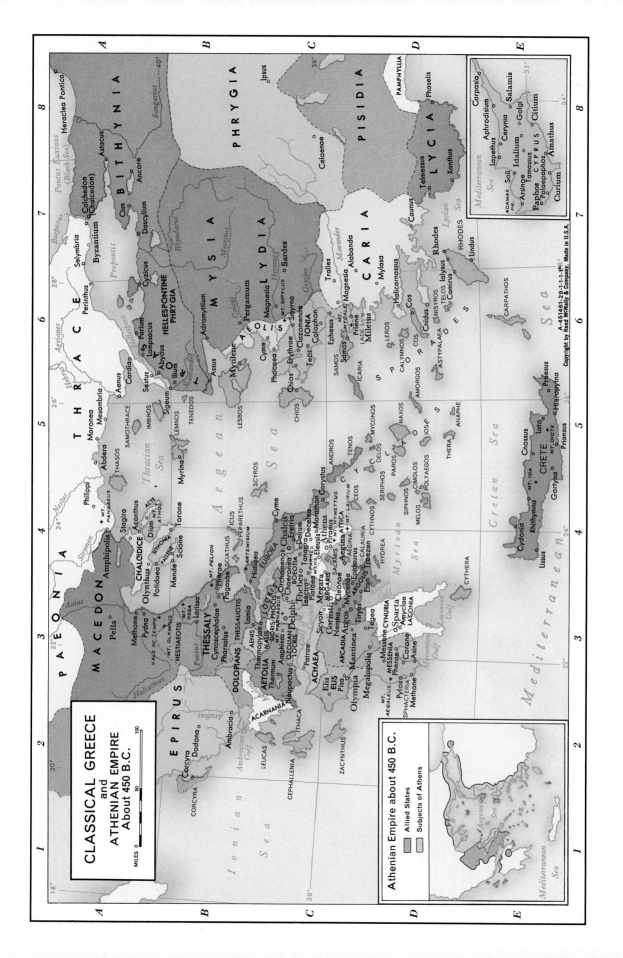

CLASSICAL GREECE
and
ATHENIAN EMPIRE
About 450 B.C.

MILES
0   50   100

Athenian Empire about 450 B.C.

Allied States

Subjects of Athens

ANCIENT PERSIA 549 B.C. – 651 A.D.

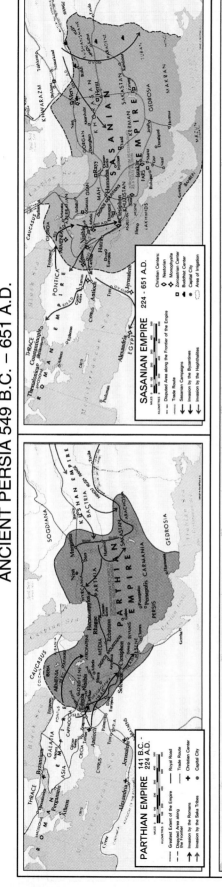

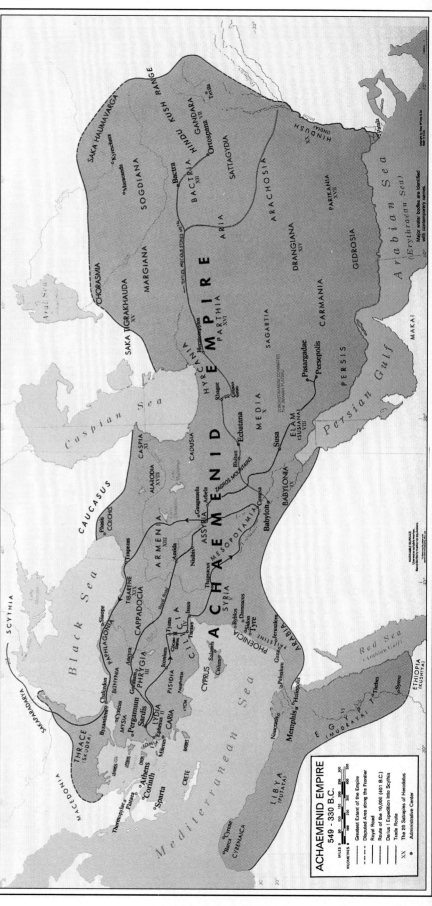

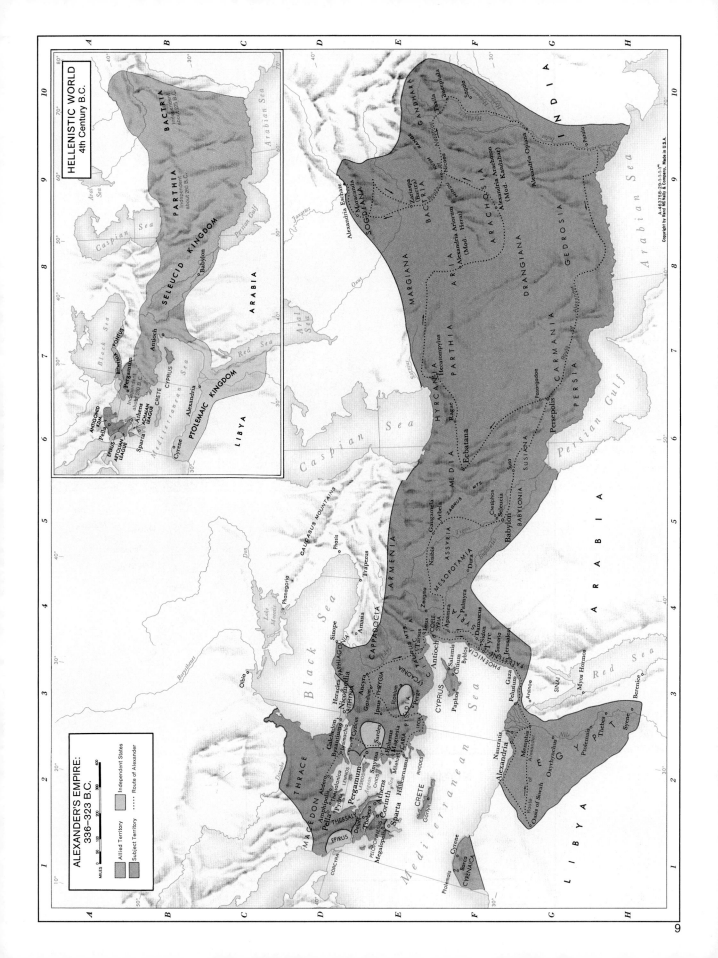

ALEXANDER'S EMPIRE:
336–323 B.C.

Allied Territory
Subject Territory
Independent States
······ Route of Alexander

MILES
0   50   100   200   300   400

HELLENISTIC WORLD
4th Century B.C.

9

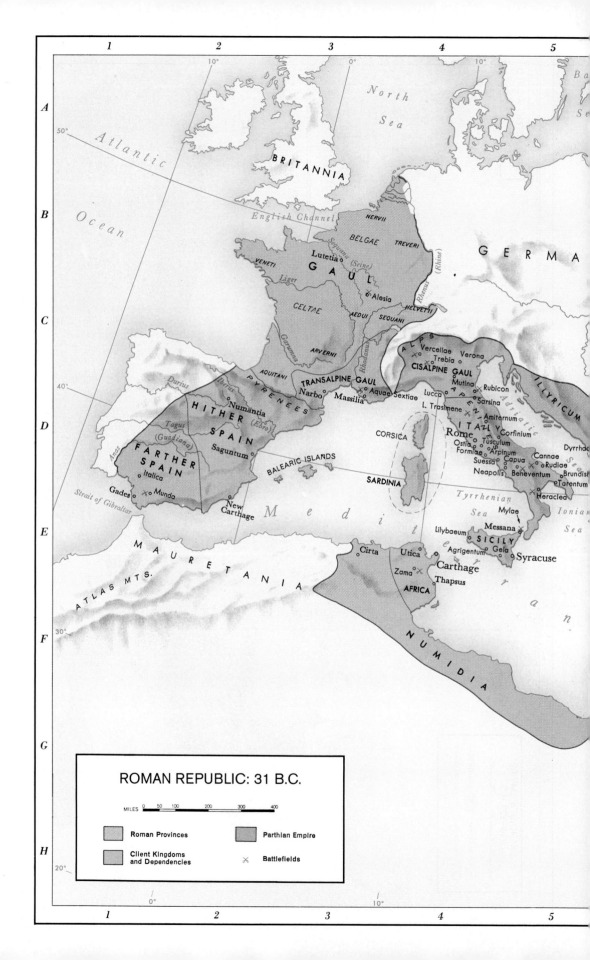

ROMAN REPUBLIC: 31 B.C.

MILES 0 50 100 200 300 400

Roman Provinces

Client Kingdoms and Dependencies

Parthian Empire

✕ Battlefields

Map labels:

North Sea

BRITANNIA

Atlantic Ocean

English Channel

GERMA...

GAUL
NERVII
BELGAE
TREVERI
VENETI
Lutetia
Sequana (Seine)
Rhenus (Rhine)
Liger
CELTAE
Alesia
AEDUI
SEQUANI
HELVETII
Garumna
ARVERNI
Rhodanus
AQUITANI
TRANSALPINE GAUL
PYRENEES
Narbo
Aquae Sextiae
Massilia

CISALPINE GAUL
ALPS
Vercellae
Trebia
Verona
Mutina
Rubicon
Lucca
Sarsina
L. Trasimene
Amiternum
ITALY
Rome
Corfinium
Ostia
Tusculum
Arpinum
Formiae
Suessa
Cannae
Capua
Neapolis
Rudiae
Beneventum
Brundisi...
Tarentum
Heraclea

ILLYRICUM
Adriatic Sea
Dyrrha...

HITHER SPAIN
Durius
Numantia
Iberus (Ebro)
Tagus (Guadiana)
Saguntum
FARTHER SPAIN
Anas
Italica
Gades
Munda
Strait of Gibraltar
New Carthage

BALEARIC ISLANDS

CORSICA

SARDINIA

Mediterranean

Tyrrhenian Sea

Mylae
Messana
SICILY
Lilybaeum
Agrigentum
Gela
Syracuse

Ionian Sea

MAURETANIA
ATLAS MTS.

Cirta
Utica
Zama
Carthage
Thapsus
AFRICA

NUMIDIA

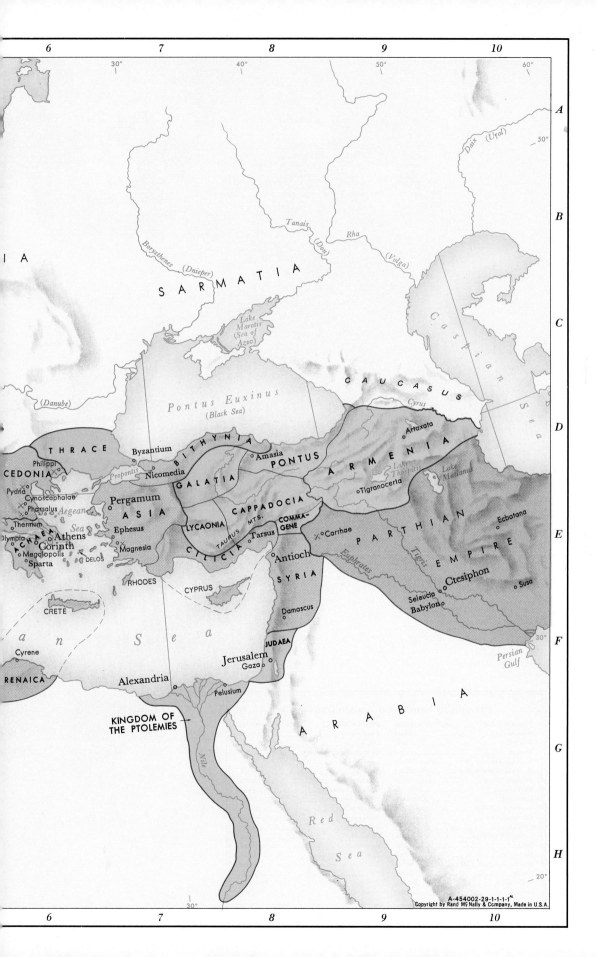

6 7 8 9 10

30° 40° 50° 60°

A

50°

Dax (Ural)

B

Tanais

Rha

Borysthenes (Dnieper)

S A R M A T I A

(Don) *(Volga)*

Caspian Sea

C

Lake Maeotis (Sea of Azov)

(Danube)

C A U C A S U S

D

Pontus Euxinus (Black Sea)

Cyrus

• Artaxata

THRACE

Byzantium

B I T H Y N I A

• Amasia

P O N T U S

A R M E N I A

• Philippi

CEDONIA

Propontis

Nicomedia

G A L A T I A

Lake Thospitis

Lake Matiana

Pydna •

Cynoscephalae

Pergamum

A S I A

C A P P A D O C I A

• Tigranocerta

• Ecbatana

Pharsalus •

Aegean

A C H A E A

Thermium

Ephesus •

L Y C A O N I A

TAURUS MTS.

COMMA-GENE

P A R T H I A N

Olympia

Athens

Sea

Tarsus

× Carrhae

E

Megalopolis •

Corinth

Magnesia

C I L I C I A

E M P I R E

Tigris

Sparta •

DELOS

Antioch •

Euphrates

Ctesiphon •

• Susa

RHODES

S Y R I A

Seleucia •

CYPRUS

Babylon •

CRETE

Damascus •

an

S *e* *a*

30°

F

Cyrene •

JUDAEA

Persian Gulf

Jerusalem •

Gaza •

RENAICA

Alexandria •

Pelusium •

A R A B I A

KINGDOM OF
THE PTOLEMIES

Nile

G

Red

H

Sea

20°

6 7 8 9 10

30°

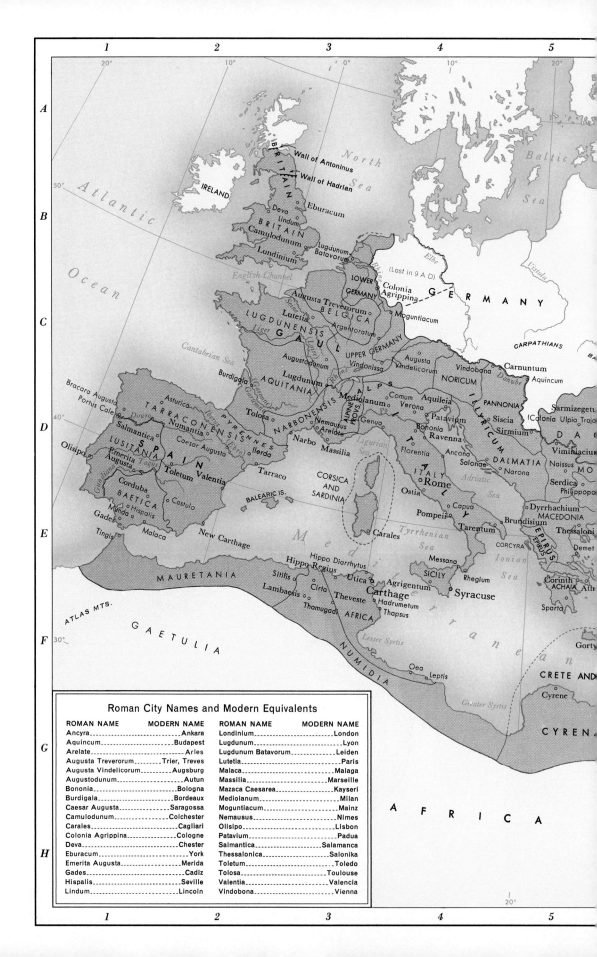

North Sea

Baltic Sea

Atlantic Ocean

IRELAND

Wall of Antoninus
Wall of Hadrian
Eburacum

BRITAIN
Deva
Lindum
Camulodunum
Londinium

English Channel

LOWER GERMANY
Colonia Agrippina
(Lost in 9 A D)
GERMANY

Augusta Treverorum
BELGICA
Lutetia
Argentoratum
Moguntiacum

Vistula

CARPATHIANS

LUGDUNENSIS GAUL
Augustodunum
Lugdunum
AQUITANIA
Burdigala

UPPER GERMANY
Vindonissa
Augusta Vindelicorum
Vindobona
NORICUM
Carnuntum
Aquincum
PANNONIA
Siscia
Sirmium
Sarmizegetu
(Colonia Ulpia Traja
ILLYRICUM

Bracara Augusta
Portus Cale
Asturica
TARRACONENSIS
SPAIN
Numantia
Salmantica
LUSITANIA
Olisipo
Emerita Augusta
Toletum
Valentia
Corduba
BAETICA
Hispalis
Munda
Gades
Malaca
Tingis

Douro
Caesar Augusta
Ilerda
PYRENEES
NARBONENSIS
Tolosa
Nemausus
Arelate
Narbo
Massilia
Tarraco
New Carthage
BALEARIC IS.

ALPS
ALPINE PROVS.
Mediolanum
Comum
Verona
Genua
Aquileia
Patavium
Bononia
Ravenna
Florentia
Ancona
Salonae
DALMATIA
Narona
Vimihiaciu
Naissus
Serdica
Philippopo

Ligurian Sea
CORSICA AND SARDINIA
ITALY
Rome
Ostia
Capua
Pompeii
Tarentum
Carales
Tyrrhenian Sea
Brundisium
MACEDONIA
Dyrrhachium
EPIRUS
CORCYRA
Thessaloni
Demet

Adriatic Sea
Ionian Sea

MAURETANIA
Sitifis
Lambaesis
ATLAS MTS.
GAETULIA

Hippo Diarrhytus
Hippo Regius
Utica
Cirta
Theveste
Thamugadi
Carthage
Hadrumetum
Thapsus
AFRICA
Messana
Agrigentum
SICILY
Syracuse
Rhegium

Corinth
ACHAIA
Sparta

Mediterranean Sea

NUMIDIA
Lesser Syrtis

CRETE AND

Oea
Leptis
Greater Syrtis

Cyrene

CYRENA

AFRICA

20° 10° 0° 10° 20°

50°

40°

30°

Roman City Names and Modern Equivalents

ROMAN NAME	MODERN NAME	ROMAN NAME	MODERN NAME
Ancyra	Ankara	Londinium	London
Aquincum	Budapest	Lugdunum	Lyon
Arelate	Arles	Lugdunum Batavorum	Leiden
Augusta Treverorum	Trier, Treves	Lutetia	Paris
Augusta Vindelicorum	Augsburg	Malaca	Malaga
Augustodunum	Autun	Massilia	Marseille
Bononia	Bologna	Mazaca Caesarea	Kayseri
Burdigala	Bordeaux	Mediolanum	Milan
Caesar Augusta	Saragossa	Moguntiacum	Mainz
Camulodunum	Colchester	Nemausus	Nimes
Carales	Cagliari	Olisipo	Lisbon
Colonia Agrippina	Cologne	Patavium	Padua
Deva	Chester	Salmantica	Salamanca
Eburacum	York	Thessalonica	Salonika
Emerita Augusta	Merida	Toletum	Toledo
Gades	Cadiz	Tolosa	Toulouse
Hispalis	Seville	Valentia	Valencia
Lindum	Lincoln	Vindobona	Vienna

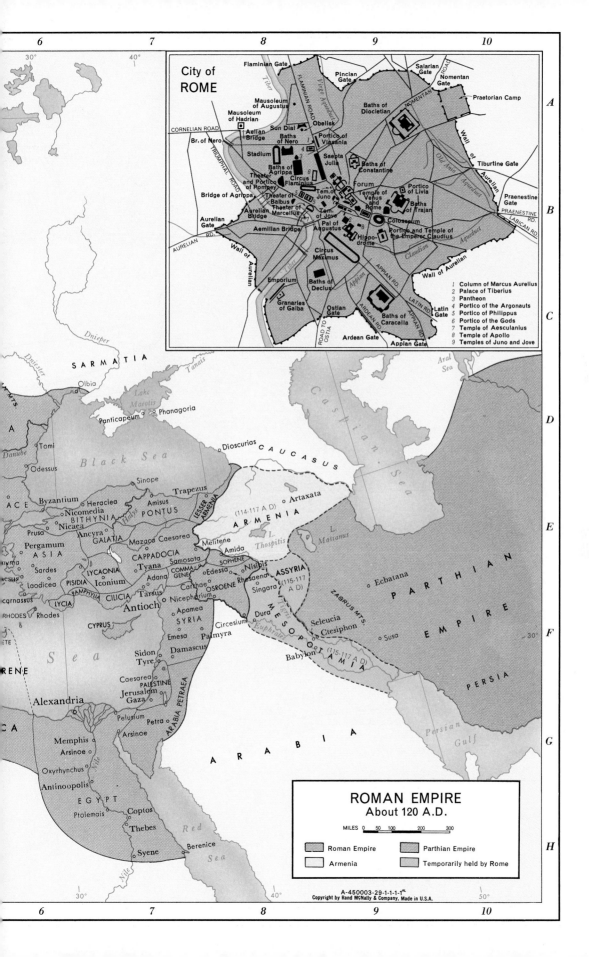

City of ROME

Flaminian Gate
Pincian Gate
Salarian Gate
Nomentan Gate
Praetorian Camp
Mausoleum of Augustus
Mausoleum of Hadrian
Baths of Diocletian
CORNELIAN ROAD
Sun Dial
Obelisk
Aelian Bridge
Br. of Nero
Baths of Nero
Portico of Vipsania
Stadium
Saepta Julia
Baths of Constantine
Baths of Agrippa
Theater and Portico of Pompey
Circus Flaminius
Tem. of Juno
Forum
Temple of Venus and Rome
Portico of Livia
Baths of Trajan
Bridge of Agrippa
Theater of Balbus
Theater of Marcellus
Tem. of Jove
Tiburtine Gate
Aurelian Gate
Aemilian Bridge
Pal of Augustus
Hippo-drome
Colosseum
Portico and Temple of the Emperor Claudius
Praenestine Gate
Wall of Aurelian
Circus Maximus
Wall of Aurelian
Emporium
Baths of Declus
Granaries of Galba
Ostian Gate
Baths of Caracalla
Latin Gate
Ardean Gate
Applan Gate

1 Column of Marcus Aurelius
2 Palace of Tiberius
3 Pantheon
4 Portico of the Argonauts
5 Portico of Philippus
6 Portico of the Gods
7 Temple of Aesculanius
8 Temple of Apollo
9 Temples of Juno and Jove

ROMAN EMPIRE
About 120 A.D.

MILES 0 50 100 200 300

	Roman Empire		Parthian Empire
	Armenia		Temporarily held by Rome

A-450003-29-1-1-1-1
Copyright by Rand McNally & Company, Made in U.S.A.

SARMATIA
Olbia
Dnieper
Dniester
Tanais
Black Sea
Lake Maeotis
Panticapeum
Phanagoria
Aral Sea
Caspian Sea
Tomi
Danube
Odessus
Sinope
Dioscurias
CAUCASUS
Byzantium
Heraclea
Trapezus
Nicomedia
Amisus
LESSER ARMENIA
(114-117 A D)
Artaxata
Prusa
Nicaea
Ancyra
PONTUS
ARMENIA
ACE
Pergamum
GALATIA
Mazaca Caesarea
Melitene
L. Thospitis
L. Matianus
ASIA
Sardes
CAPPADOCIA
Amida
Ecbatana
Smyrna
LYCAONIA
Tyana
SOPHENE
PARTHIAN
Laodicea
PISIDIA
Iconium
COMMA GENE
Samosata
Edessa
Nisibis
ASSYRIA
(115-117 A D)
csus
PAMPHYLIA
CILICIA
Tarsus
Adana
OSROENE
Carthae
Rhesaena
Singara
ZAGRUS MTS.
EMPIRE
carnassus
LYCIA
Antioch
Nicepherium
Dura
Seleucia
RHODES
Rhodes
Apamea
MESOPOTAMIA
Ctesiphon
Susa
CYPRUS
SYRIA
Circesium
Euphrates
PERSIA
Sea
Emesa
Palmyra
Seleucia
(115-117 A D)
CRETE
Sidon
Damascus
Babylon
Tyre
RENE
Caesarea
PALESTINE
Jerusalem
Gaza
Alexandria
Pelusium
Petra
ARABIA PETRAEA
A R A B I A
Persian Gulf
CA
Memphis
Arsinoe
Arsinoe
Oxyrhynchus
Antinoopolis
Nile
E G Y P T
Ptolemais
Coptos
Red
Thebes
Syene
Berenice
Sea

30°   40°   50°

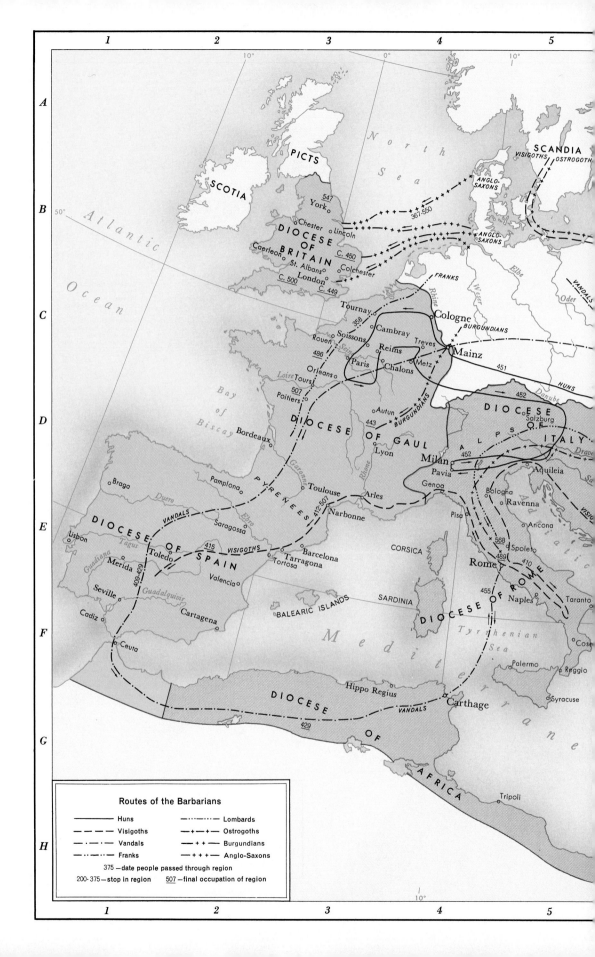

Routes of the Barbarians

——————	Huns	—·····—·····—	Lombards
— — — —	Visigoths	—+—+—+—	Ostrogoths
—·—··—·—··—	Vandals	+ + +	Burgundians
—·—·—·—·—	Franks	+ + +	Anglo-Saxons

375 —date people passed through region

200-375 —stop in region   507 —final occupation of region

Map labels

PICTS

SCOTIA

SCANDIA

VISIGOTHS   OSTROGOTH

ANGLO-SAXONS

North Sea

547
York

Chester   Lincoln

DIOCESE OF BRITAIN

Caerleon
St. Albans
London   Colchester
C. 500   C. 450
C. 449

367-550

ANGLO-SAXONS

VANDALS

Atlantic Ocean

50°

FRANKS

Tournay   Cologne
BURGUNDIANS

Cambray   Treves   Mainz
Soissons   Reims
Rouen   Metz   451
Seine   Chalons
Paris
Orleans
Loire   Tours
507   Poitiers

Bay of Biscay

Bordeaux

DIOCESE OF GAUL

Autun
443
BURGUNDIANS

Lyon

Rhone

452   Danube   HUNS

DIOCESE OF ITALY

Salzburg   Drave

452   Milan
Pavia   Aquileia
Genoa   Bologna
Pisa   Ravenna
Ancona
568
Spoleto
489   410
Rome
455   Naples   Taranto

VISIG

Braga   Pamplona
Duero   PYRENEES   Toulouse
412-507   Arles
VANDALS   Saragossa   Narbonne
Ebro
415   VISIGOTHS   Barcelona
Lisbon   Toledo   Tortosa
Tagus   Valencia
409-429   Merida   DIOCESE OF SPAIN   Cartagena
Guadiana   Seville
Guadalquivir
Cadiz

Ceuta

CORSICA

SARDINIA

BALEARIC ISLANDS

Mediterranean Sea

Tyrrhenian Sea

DIOCESE OF ROME

Palermo   Cose
Reggio
Syracuse

DIOCESE OF AFRICA

Hippo Regius   Carthage
VANDALS
429

Tripoli

10°   0°   10°

10°

Drave   Sa

Oder   Elbe   Weser   Rhine

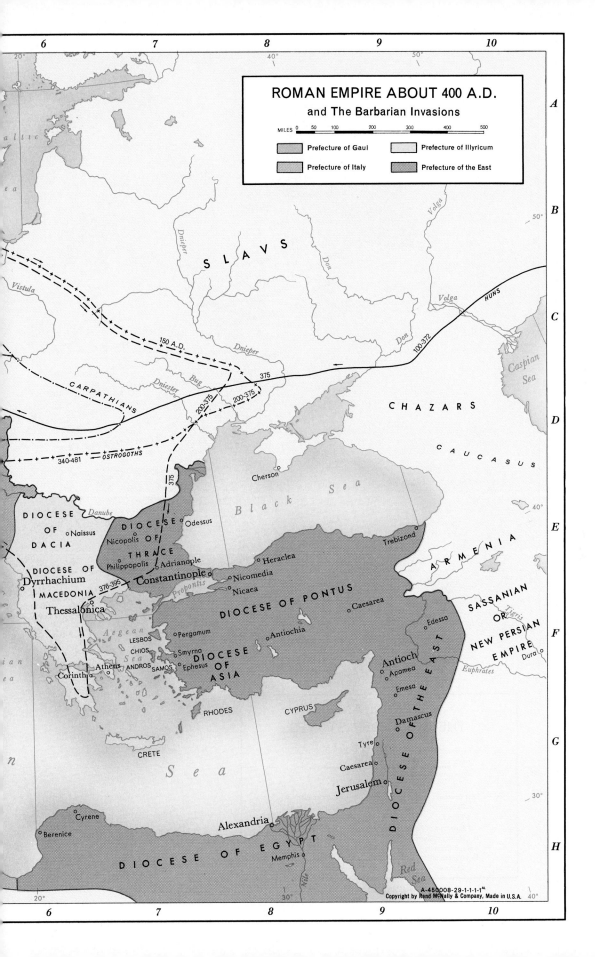

ROMAN EMPIRE ABOUT 400 A.D.
and The Barbarian Invasions

MILES 0 50 100 200 300 400 500

Prefecture of Gaul

Prefecture of Italy

Prefecture of Illyricum

Prefecture of the East

Baltic Sea

Vistula

S L A V S

Dnieper

Don

Volga

Volga

HUNS

50°

Dnieper

150 A.D.

375

CARPATHIANS

Dniester *Bug*

200-375   200-375

340-481   OSTROGOTHS

100-372

Don

C H A Z A R S

Caspian Sea

C A U C A S U S

40°

Cherson

Black   Sea

A R M E N I A

DIOCESE
OF
DACIA

Danube

○ Naissus

DIOCESE
OF
THRACE

Nicopolis

Odessus ○

Trebizond ○

SASSANIAN
OR
NEW PERSIAN
EMPIRE

DIOCESE OF
MACEDONIA

Dyrrhachium

Philippopolis ○   Adrianople ○

376-395   Constantinople ○

Heraclea ○

Nicomedia ○

Nicaea ○

DIOCESE OF PONTUS

Tigris

Edessa ○

Dura ○

Thessalonica

Propontis

Pergamum ○

Aegean   Sea

LESBOS

CHIOS

Athens ○   SAMOS

Corinth ○   ANDROS

Smyrna ○

Ephesus ○

DIOCESE
OF
ASIA

Antiochia ○

Caesarea ○

Euphrates

Antioch ○

Apamea ○

Emesa ○

Damascus ○

DIOCESE OF THE EAST

RHODES

CYPRUS

CRETE

Sea

Tyre ○

Caesarea ○

Jerusalem ○

30°

Cyrene ○

Berenice ○

Alexandria ○

DIOCESE   OF   EGYPT

Memphis ○

Nile

Red Sea

A-450008-29-1-1-1-1 AL
Copyright by Rand McNally & Company, Made in U.S.A.

40°

20°

30°

15

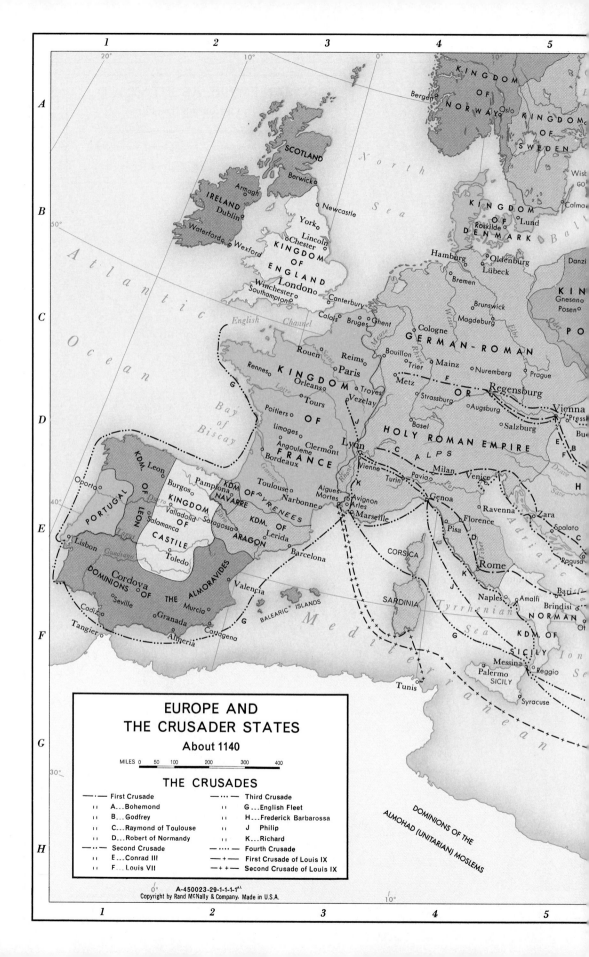

EUROPE AND THE CRUSADER STATES

About 1140

MILES 0 50 100   200   300   400

THE CRUSADES

—·— First Crusade	—··— Third Crusade
͞ A...Bohemond	͞ G...English Fleet
͞ B...Godfrey	͞ H...Frederick Barbarossa
͞ C...Raymond of Toulouse	͞ J...Philip
͞ D...Robert of Normandy	͞ K...Richard
—·—· Second Crusade	—···· Fourth Crusade
͞ E...Conrad III	—+— First Crusade of Louis IX
͞ F...Louis VII	—+—+ Second Crusade of Louis IX

A-450023-29-1-1-1-1^AL
Copyright by Rand McNally & Company. Made in U.S.A.

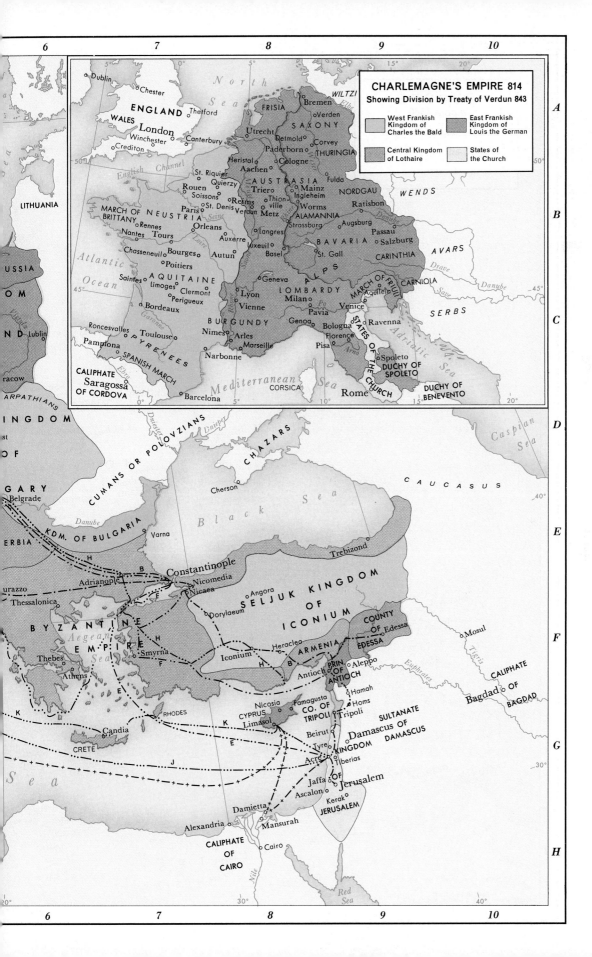

CHARLEMAGNE'S EMPIRE 814
Showing Division by Treaty of Verdun 843

West Frankish Kingdom of Charles the Bald
Central Kingdom of Lothaire
East Frankish Kingdom of Louis the German
States of the Church

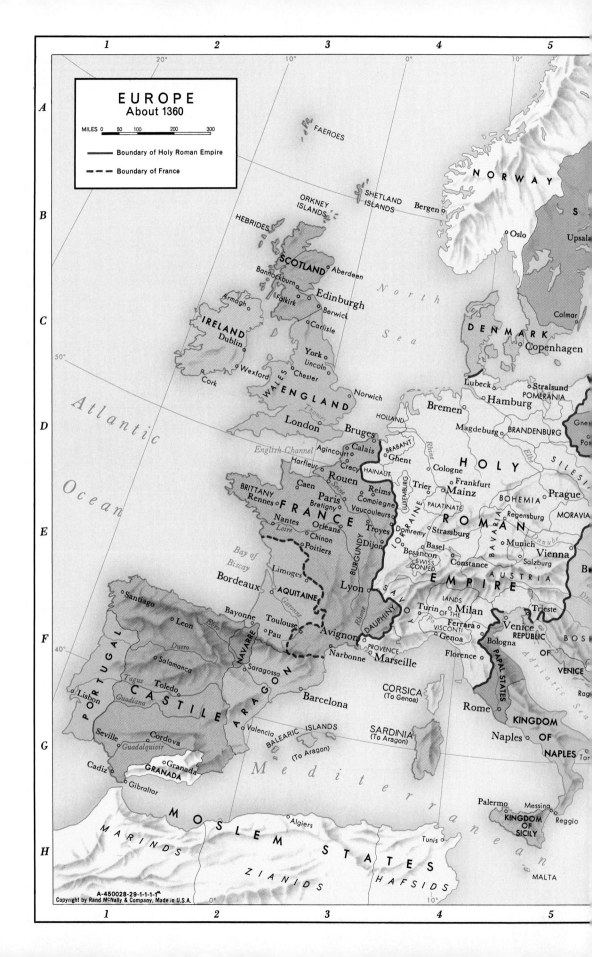

EUROPE
About 1360

MILES 0 50 100 200 300

―――― Boundary of Holy Roman Empire

‑ ‑ ‑ ‑ Boundary of France

Atlantic Ocean

FAEROES

NORWAY

SHETLAND ISLANDS
Bergen
ORKNEY ISLANDS
Oslo
HEBRIDES
Upsala

North Sea

SCOTLAND
Aberdeen
Bannockburn
Falkirk
Edinburgh
Berwick
Armagh
Carlisle
IRELAND
Dublin
York
Lincoln
Wexford
Chester
Cork
WALES ENGLAND
Norwich

DENMARK
Copenhagen
Calmar

Lubeck
Stralsund
POMERANIA
Hamburg
Bremen
HOLLAND
Magdeburg
BRANDENBURG
Gnes
Pos

London
Bruges
Thames
Ghent
BRABANT
Rhine
HOLY
SILESI
English Channel
Agincourt
Calais
HAINAUT
Cologne
Frankfurt
Prague
Harfleur
Crecy
LUXEMBURG
Trier
Mainz
BOHEMIA
Rouen
Reims
ROMAN
MORAVIA
Caen
Paris
Compiegne
PALATINATE
Regensburg
BRITTANY
Bretigny
Vaucouleurs
LORRAINE
Rennes
Orleans
Troyes
Domremy
Strassburg
BAVARIA
Munich
Vienna
FRANCE
Chinon
Dijon
Besancon
Basel
AUSTRIA
Salzburg
Nantes
Poitiers
BURGUNDY
Constance
B
Loire
SWISS CONFED
EMPIRE
Bay of Biscay
Limoges
Lyon
SAVOY
Turin
Milan
Trieste
Bordeaux
LANDS OF THE
Po
AQUITAINE
Garonne
DAUPHINY
Ferrara
Venice
VISCONTI
Santiago
Bayonne
Toulouse
Avignon
Genoa
Bologna
REPUBLIC
Leon
NAVARRE
Pau
PROVENCE
Florence
OF
PORTUGAL
Salamanca
Saragossa
Narbonne
Marseille
PAPAL STATES
VENICE
Duero
Toledo
ARAGON
Barcelona
CORSICA
(To Genoa)
Rome
Rag
Lisbon
CASTILE
Tagus
Guadiana
Valencia
BALEARIC ISLANDS
SARDINIA
(To Aragon)
KINGDOM
Seville
Cordova
(To Aragon)
Naples
OF
Cadiz
GRANADA
Granada
NAPLES
Tar
Guadalquivir
Gibraltar
Mediterranean
Palermo
Messing
KINGDOM
Reggio
OF SICILY
MARINDS
Algiers
MOSLEM STATES
MALTA
ZIANIDS
Tunis
HAFSIDS

Adriatic Sea
BOS

A-450028-29-1-1-1-T
Copyright by Rand McNally & Company, Made in U.S.A.

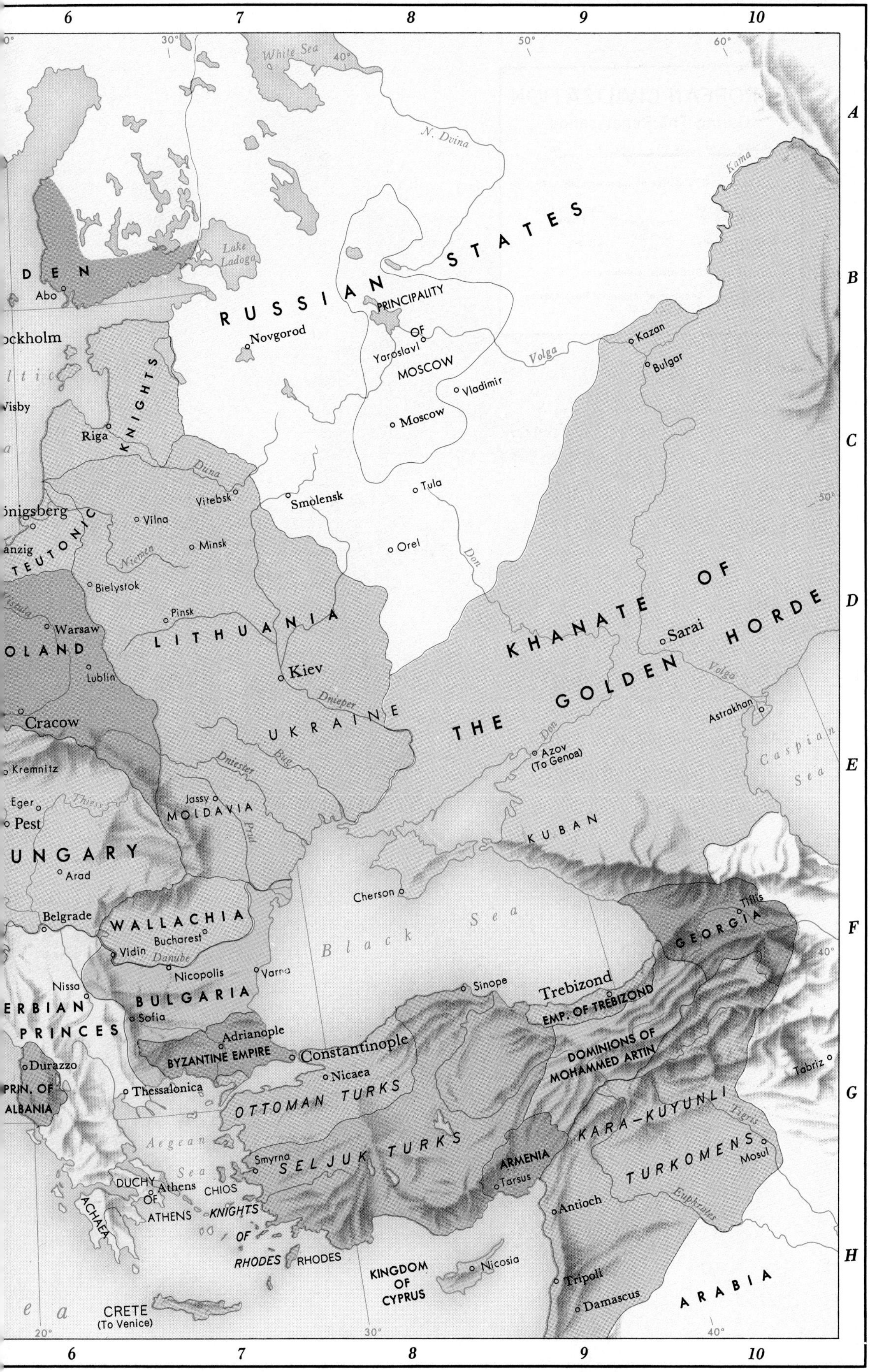

RUSSIAN STATES
PRINCIPALITY OF MOSCOW
Novgorod
Yaroslavl
Vladimir
Moscow
Smolensk
Tula
Orel
Vitebsk
Vilna
Minsk
Pinsk
Kiev
LITHUANIA
UKRAINE
KHANATE OF THE GOLDEN HORDE
Kazan
Bulgar
Sarai
Astrakhan
Azov
(To Genoa)
KUBAN
Caspian Sea
Black Sea
Cherson
MOLDAVIA
Jassy
WALLACHIA
Bucharest
Vidin
Nicopolis
Varna
BULGARIA
Sofia
Adrianople
BYZANTINE EMPIRE
Constantinople
Nicaea
OTTOMAN TURKS
SELJUK TURKS
Smyrna
Thessalonica
PRIN. OF ALBANIA
Durazzo
ERBIAN PRINCES
Nissa
Belgrade
UNGARY
Arad
Pest
Eger
Kremnitz
Cracow
OLAND
Warsaw
Lublin
Bielystok
TEUTONIC KNIGHTS
önigsberg
anzig
Riga
Visby
ockholm
Abo
DEN
Lake Ladoga
White Sea
N. Dvina
Kama
Volga
Don
Dnieper
Dniester
Bug
Prut
Danube
Thiess
Niemen
Vistula
Düna
GEORGIA
Tiflis
Trebizond
EMP. OF TREBIZOND
Sinope
DOMINIONS OF MOHAMMED ARTIN
KARA-KUYUNLI
TURKOMENS
Mosul
Tabriz
Tigris
Euphrates
ARMENIA
Tarsus
Antioch
Tripoli
Damascus
ARABIA
KINGDOM OF CYPRUS
Nicosia
KNIGHTS OF RHODES
RHODES
CHIOS
DUCHY OF ATHENS
Athens
ACHAEA
Aegean Sea
CRETE
(To Venice)

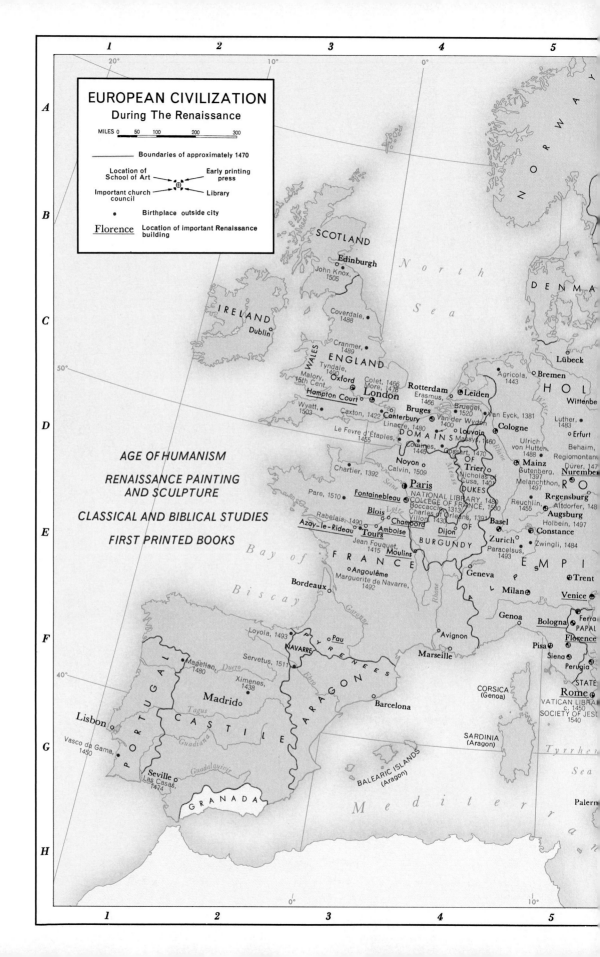

EUROPEAN CIVILIZATION
During The Renaissance

MILES 0 50 100 200 300

_____ Boundaries of approximately 1470

Location of — ⊕ — Early printing
School of Art   press

Important church — ⊕ — Library
council

● Birthplace outside city

<u>Florence</u> Location of important Renaissance
building

AGE OF HUMANISM

*RENAISSANCE PAINTING
AND SCULPTURE*

CLASSICAL AND BIBLICAL STUDIES

FIRST PRINTED BOOKS

NORWAY

DENMAR

SCOTLAND
Edinburgh
John Knox,
1505

North

Sea

IRELAND
Dublin

Coverdale,
1488

Lübeck

WALES ENGLAND
Cranmer,
1489
Tyndale,
1490
Malory, Oxford Colet, 1466
15th Cent.   More, 1478
Hampton Court London
Wyatt, Caxton, 1422 Canterbury
1503
Linacre, 1480

Rotterdam
Erasmus,
1466

Agricola,
1443
Bremen

HOL

Leiden
Wittenbe
Bruges Van der Wyden
Van Eyck, 1381 Luther,
Bruegel, 1400   1483
1520 DOMAINS Louvain Cologne Erfurt
Le Fevre d'Étaples, Massys, 1460
1455 Commes, Ulrich Behaim,
1448 Ossart, 1470 von Hutten, Regiomontan
Noyon OF 1488 Dürer, 147
Chartier, 1392 Calvin, 1509 Trier Mainz Nuremberg
Nicholas of Gutenberg, Melanchthon,
Pare, 1510 Paris DUKES Cusa, 140 1455 1497
NATIONAL LIBRARY, 1480 R O
Fontainebleau COLLEGE OF FRANCE, 1530 Reuchlin, Regensburg
Boccaccio, 1313 1455 Altdorfer, 148
Blois Charles of Orleans, 139 Augsburg
Rabelais, 1490 Villon, 1430 Basel Holbein, 1497
Azay-le-Rideau Chambord Zurich Constance
Tours Amboise Dijon OF Zwingli, 1484
Jean Fouquet, BURGUNDY Paracelsus,
1415 Moulins Geneva 1493 E M P I
FRANCE Trent
Angoulême Milan
Marguerite de Navarre, Po
1492 Venice
Bordeaux Genoa
Bologna Ferra
Loyola, 1493 Pau Pisa PAPAL
NAVARRE Avignon Florence
Servetus, 1511 Siena
Magellan, PYRENEES Marseille Perugia
1480 Duero CORSICA
Ximenes, (Genoa) STATE
1438 Rome
Madrid VATICAN LIBRA
PORTUGAL CASTILE ARAGON c. 1450
Barcelona SOCIETY OF JESU
Lisbon Tagus 1540
Vasco da Gama, SARDINIA
1450 Guadiana (Aragon) Tyrrhen
Seville Sea
Las Casas, Guadalquivir
1474 BALEARIC ISLANDS
GRANADA (Aragon) Palern

Bay of

Biscay

AGE OF HUMANISM

Mediterran

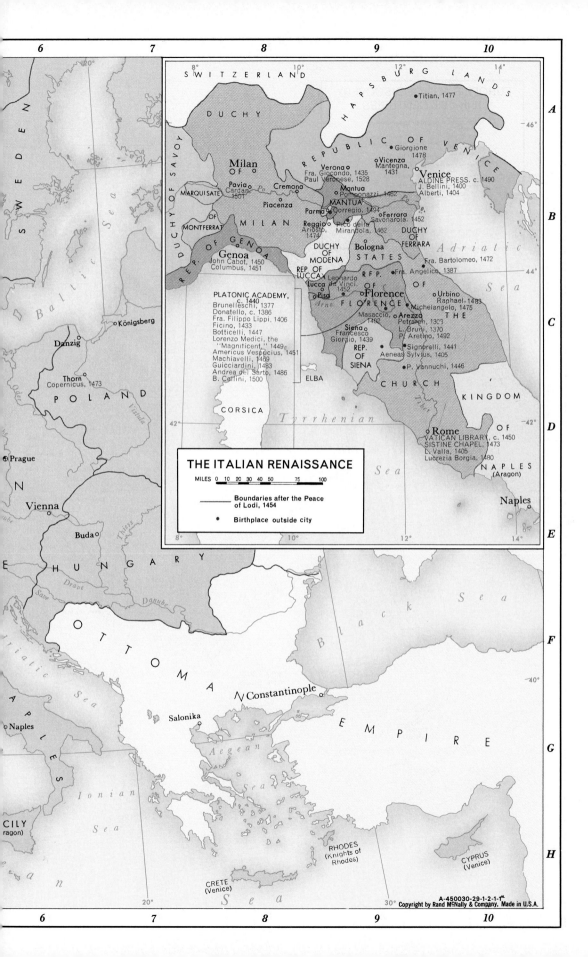

THE ITALIAN RENAISSANCE

MILES 0 10 20 30 40 50 75 100

Boundaries after the Peace of Lodi, 1454

• Birthplace outside city

PLATONIC ACADEMY, c. 1440
Brunelleschi, 1377
Donatello, c. 1386
Fra. Filippo Lippi, 1406
Ficino, 1433
Botticelli, 1447
Lorenzo Medici, the "Magnificent," 1449
Americus Vespucius, 1451
Machiavelli, 1469
Guicciardini, 1483
Andrea del Sarto, 1486
B. Cellini, 1500

Titian, 1477

Giorgione, 1478

Vicenza
Mantegna, 1431

Verona
Fra. Giocondo, 1435
Paul Veronese, 1528

Venice
ALDINE PRESS, c. 1490
J. Bellini, 1400
Alberti, 1404

Milan

Pavia
Cardan, 1501

Cremona

Piacenza

Mantua
Pomponazzi, 1462

Parma
Correggio, 1494

Reggio
Ariosto, 1474

Pico della Mirandola, 1462

Ferrara
Savonarola, 1452

DUCHY OF FERRARA

DUCHY OF MODENA

Genoa
John Cabot, 1450
Columbus, 1451

Bologna

STATES

Fra. Bartolomeo, 1472

REP. OF LUCCA

Lucca

Leonardo da Vinci, 1452

Fra. Angelico, 1387

Pisa

Florence

Masaccio, 1402

Arezzo
Petrarch, 1303
L. Bruni, 1370
P. Aretino, 1492

Urbino
Raphael, 1483

Michelangelo, 1475

Siena
Francesco Giorgio, 1439

REP. OF SIENA

Aeneas Sylvius, 1405

Signorelli, 1441

P. Vannuchi, 1446

ELBA

CORSICA

Tyrrhenian

CHURCH

KINGDOM

Rome
VATICAN LIBRARY, c. 1450
SISTINE CHAPEL, 1473
L. Valla, 1405
Lucrezia Borgia, 1480

OF

NAPLES
(Aragon)

Naples

Sea

SWITZERLAND

HAPSBURG LANDS

DUCHY OF SAVOY

MARQUISATE OF MONTFERRAT

REP. OF GENOA

DUCHY OF MILAN

REPUBLIC OF VENICE

Adriatic Sea

Baltic Sea

SWEDEN

Königsberg

Danzig

Thorn
Copernicus, 1473

POLAND

Prague

Vienna

Buda

HUNGARY

Drave

Save

Danube

OTTOMAN EMPIRE

Black Sea

Constantinople

Salonika

Aegean Sea

Ionian Sea

NAPLES

Naples

SICILY
(Aragon)

CRETE
(Venice)

RHODES
(Knights of Rhodes)

CYPRUS
(Venice)

A-450030-29-1-2-1-1
Copyright by Rand McNally & Company. Made in U.S.A.

21

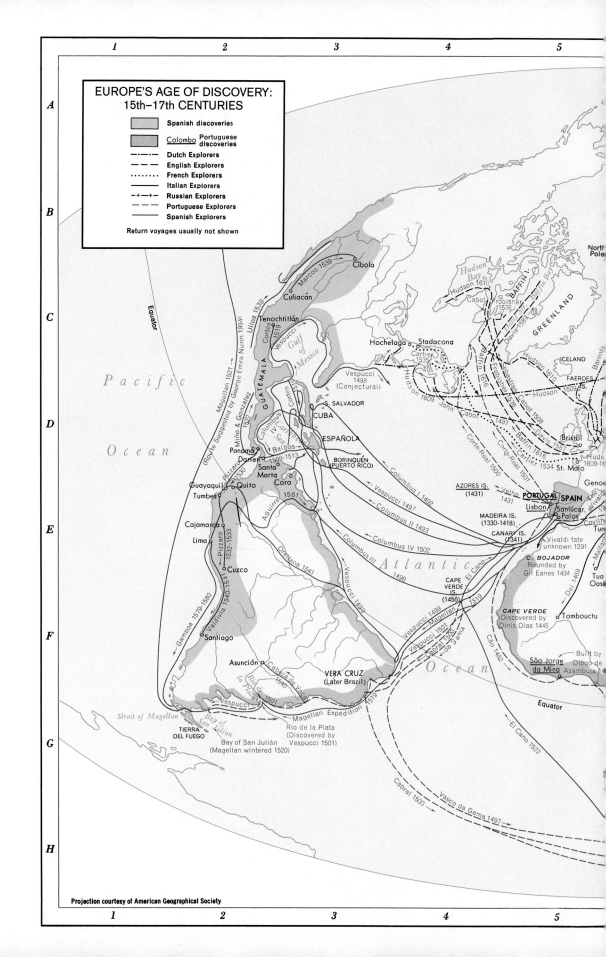

EUROPE'S AGE OF DISCOVERY: 15th–17th CENTURIES

- Spanish discoveries
- _Colombo_ Portuguese discoveries
- —·—·— Dutch Explorers
- — — — English Explorers
- ·········· French Explorers
- ———— Italian Explorers
- —+—+— Russian Explorers
- – – – Portuguese Explorers
- ———— Spanish Explorers

Return voyages usually not shown

Projection courtesy of American Geographical Society

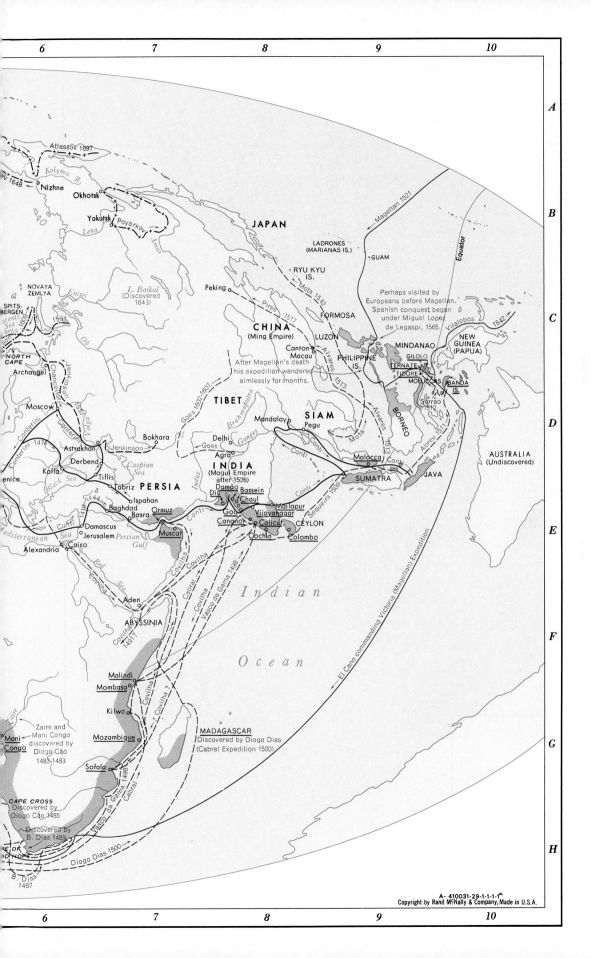

6   **7**   **8**   **9**   **10**

A

Atlassov 1697
Kolyma R.
~V 1648
Nizhne
Okhotsk
B
Yakutsk
Poyarkov
Lena
Amur
JAPAN

LADRONES
(MARIANAS IS.)
GUAM
Magellan 1521

Equator

NOVAYA
ZEMLYA
SPITS-
BERGEN
L. Baikal
(Discovered
1643)
Peking
RYU KYU
IS.
Mota 1542
FORMOSA
Perhaps visited by
Europeans before Magellan.
Spanish conquest began
under Miguel Lopez
de Legaspi, 1565.
Vitalobos
1542
C
Enisei
*Barents
Sea*
Ob
NORTH
CAPE
Archangel
Chancelor
Jenkinson
CHINA
(Ming Empire)
Pires
1517
Canton
Macau
LUZON
PHILIPPINE
IS.
MINDANAO
GILOLO
NEW
GUINEA
(PAPUA)
TERNATE
TIDORE
MOLUCCAS
After Magellan's death
his expedition wandered
aimlessly for months.
Alvares
1513
BANDA
IS.
Moscow
Volga
Jenkinson
TIBET
Brahmaputra
Goes 1602-1607
BORNEO
Serrao
1512
D
Conterini
Conterini 1474
Astrakhan
Derbend
*Caspian
Sea*
Bokhara
Delhi
Goes
Ganges
Mandalay
Pegu
SIAM
Conti
Mota
Abreu 1511
AUSTRALIA
(Undiscovered)
Kaffa
Black Sea
Tiflis
Tabriz
PERSIA
Agra
INDIA
(Mogul Empire
after 1526)
Conti
Malocca
Conti
JAVA
Venice
1419
Baghdad
Ispahan
Damão
Diu
Bassein
Chaul
SUMATRA
1444
Basra
Ormuz
Goa
Mailapur
Vijayanagar
Sequeira 1509
E
Damascus
Jerusalem
*Persian
Gulf*
Muscat
Cananor
Calicut
CEYLON
Mediterranean Sea
Cairo
Alexandria
Cochin
Colombo

Conti
Conti

I n d i a n

Covilha
Covilha
Covilha
Cabral
Vasco da Gama 1498
Covilha

Aden
F
Covilha
1497
ABYSSINIA

O c e a n

El Cano commanding Victoria (Magellan) Expedition

Malindi
Mombasa
Covilha ?
Kilwa
MADAGASCAR
Discovered by Diogo Dias
(Cabral Expedition 1500)
G
Zaire and
Mani Congo
discovered by
Diogo Cão
1482-1483
Mani
Congo
Mozambique

Sofala

CAPE CROSS
Discovered by
Diogo Cão 1485
Vasco da Gama 1498
Cabral
H
Discovered by
B. Dias 1489
Diogo Dias 1500
B. Dias
1487

A- 410031-29-1-1-1-1
Copyright by Rand McNally & Company, Made in U.S.A.

6   **7**   **8**   **9**   **10**

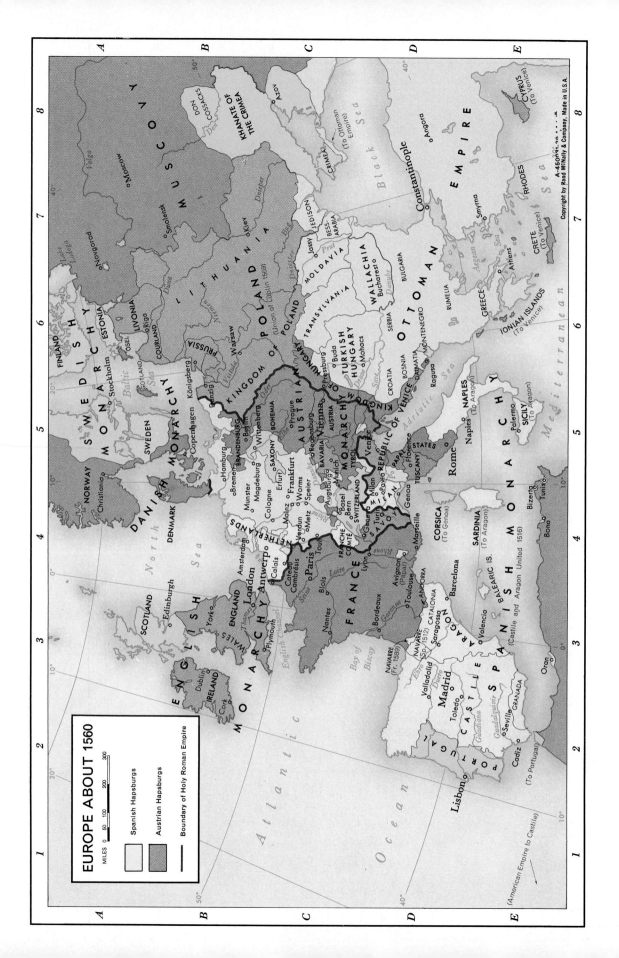

EUROPE ABOUT 1560

MILES
0   50 100   200   300

Spanish Hapsburgs
Austrian Hapsburgs
—— Boundary of Holy Roman Empire

MUSCOVY

SWEDISH MONARCHY

NORWAY

FINLAND

ESTONIA

LIVONIA

COURLAND

OSEL

GOTLAND

SWEDEN

Christiania

Stockholm

DANISH MONARCHY

DENMARK

Copenhagen

Novgorod

Moscow

Smolensk

Kiev

LITHUANIA

PRUSSIA

Königsberg

Danzig

Warsaw

KINGDOM OF POLAND

POLAND

Union of Lublin 1569

DON COSSACKS

KHANATE OF THE CRIMEA

CRIMEA (To Ottoman Empire)

Azov

Black Sea

BESS. ARABIA

JEDISON

Jassy

MOLDAVIA

TRANSYLVANIA

TURKISH HUNGARY

Buda

Pressburg

Mohacs

WALLACHIA

Bucharest

BULGARIA

SERBIA

BOSNIA

CROATIA

DALMATIA

MONTENEGRO

Ragusa

RUMELIA

OTTOMAN EMPIRE

Constantinople

Angora

Smyrna

GREECE

Athens

IONIAN ISLANDS (To Venice)

Aegean Sea

RHODES

CRETE (To Venice)

CYPRUS (To Venice)

Mediterranean Sea

AUSTRIAN MONARCHY

HUNGARY

AUSTRIA

Vienna

Prague

BOHEMIA

SAXONY

Wittenberg

Regensburg

BAVARIA

Munich

TYROL

KINGDOM OF VENICE

REPUBLIC OF VENICE

Venice

Adriatic Sea

PAPAL STATES

Florence

TUSCANY

Rome

NAPLES

Naples

SICILY (To Aragon)

Palermo

MILAN

Milan

Genoa

SWITZERLAND

Bern

Basel

Geneva

SAVOY

Turin

FRANCHE COMTÉ

Marseille

CORSICA (To Genoa)

SARDINIA (To Aragon)

Bizerta

Tunis

Bona

SPANISH MONARCHY

(Castile and Aragon United 1516)

BALEARIC IS.

Barcelona

CATALONIA

ARAGON

Saragossa

Valencia

NAVARRE Sp. (1512)

NAVARRE (Fr. 1589)

CASTILE

Madrid

Valladolid

Toledo

GRANADA

Seville

Cadiz

Oran

PORTUGAL

Lisbon

Ebro

Duero

Guadalquivir

Guadiana

ANDORRA

Toulouse

Bordeaux

Garonne

Bay of Biscay

FRANCE

Paris

Blois

Nantes

Loire

Seine

Lyon

Rhône

Avignon (Papal)

Geneva

Toul

Metz

Verdun

Mainz

Worms

Speier

Strasbourg

NETHERLANDS

Antwerp

Amsterdam

Calais

Cateau Cambrésis

Cologne

Münster

Magdeburg

Erfurt

Frankfurt

BRANDENBURG

Berlin

Hamburg

Bremen

Hanover

Danube

Rhine

ENGLISH MONARCHY

ENGLAND

London

Thames

Plymouth

York

WALES

SCOTLAND

Edinburgh

IRELAND

Dublin

Cork

English Channel

North Sea

Baltic Sea

Atlantic Ocean

Volga

Don

Dnieper

Dniester

Bug

Vistula

Oder

Elbe

Weser

Prut

Save

Drave

Duna

Niemen

(American Empire to Castile)

(To Portugal)

A-450...

Copyright by Rand McNally & Company. Made in U.S.A.

24

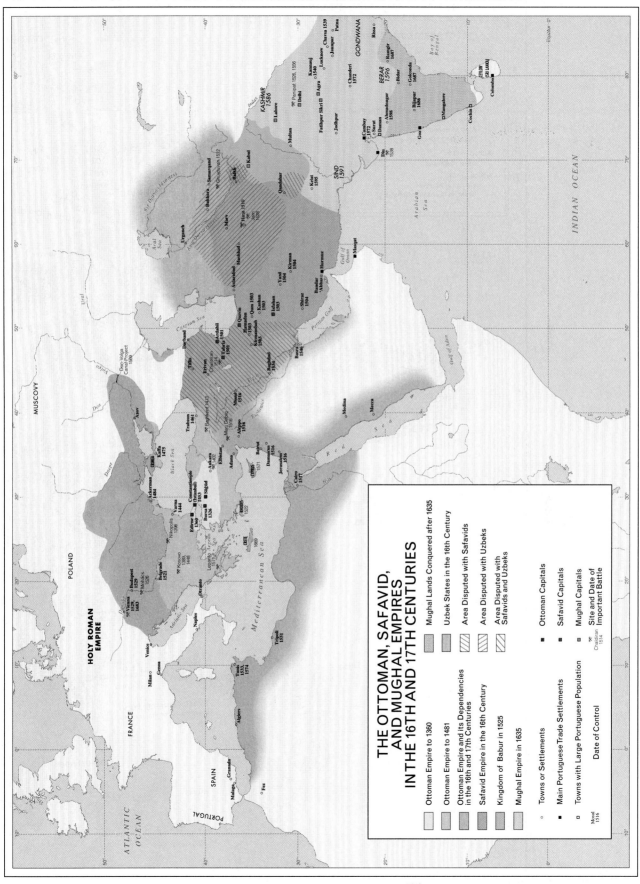

THE OTTOMAN, SAFAVID,
AND MUGHAL EMPIRES
IN THE 16TH AND 17TH CENTURIES

Ottoman Empire to 1360

Ottoman Empire to 1481

Ottoman Empire and its Dependencies
in the 16th and 17th Centuries

Safavid Empire in the 16th Century

Kingdom of Babur in 1525

Mughal Empire in 1635

Mughal Lands Conquered after 1635

Uzbek States in the 16th Century

Area Disputed with Safavids

Area Disputed with Uzbeks

Area Disputed with
Safavids and Uzbeks

■ Ottoman Capitals

■ Safavid Capitals

▣ Mughal Capitals

⚔ Chaldiran Site and Date of
1514 Important Battle

○ Towns or Settlements

■ Main Portuguese Trade Settlements

▫ Towns with Large Portuguese Population

Mosul Date of Control
1516

25

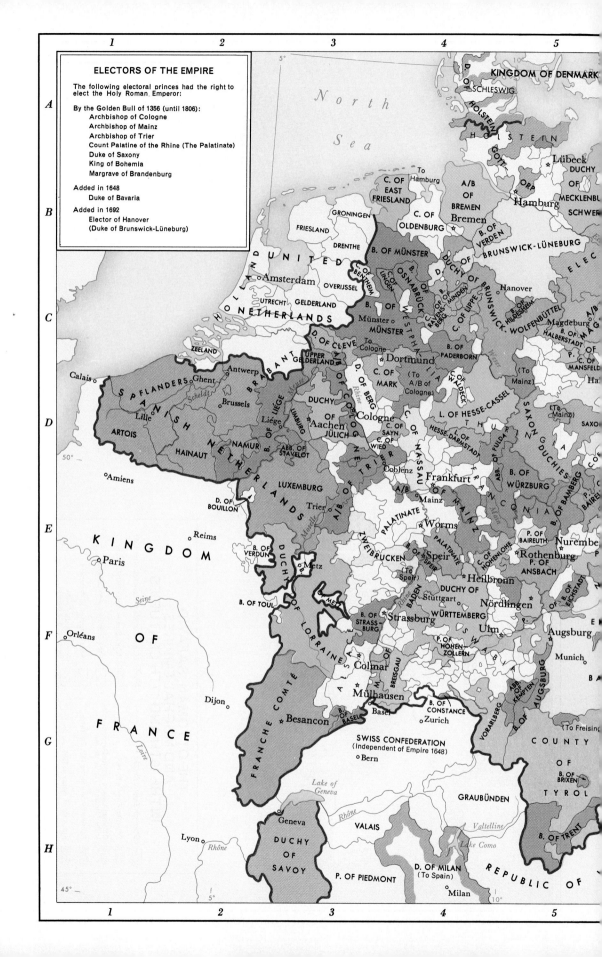

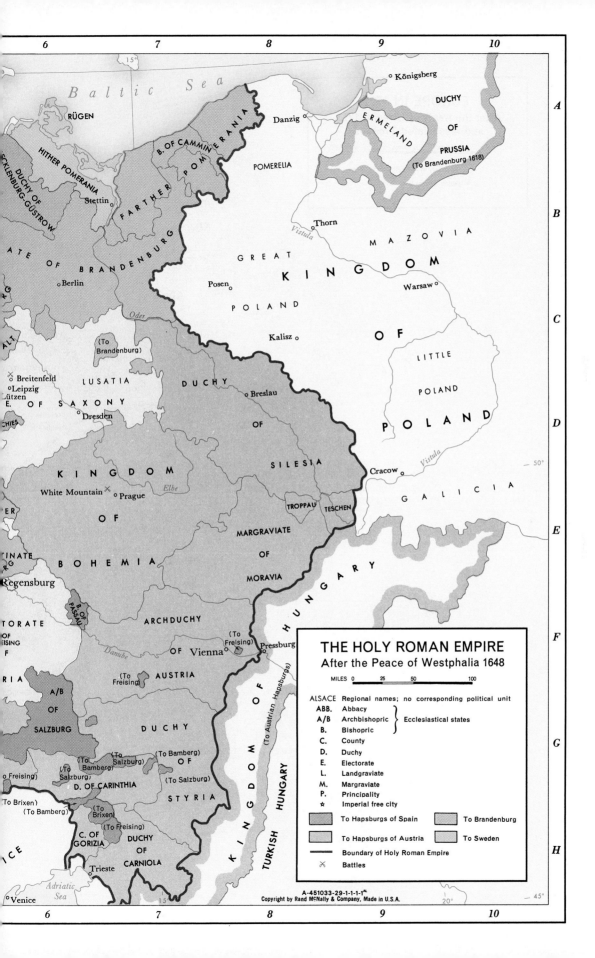

THE HOLY ROMAN EMPIRE
After the Peace of Westphalia 1648

MILES 0 — 25 — 50 — 100

ALSACE Regional names; no corresponding political unit
ABB. Abbacy ⎫
A/B Archbishopric ⎬ Ecclesiastical states
B. Bishopric ⎭
C. County
D. Duchy
E. Electorate
L. Landgraviate
M. Margraviate
P. Principality
☆ Imperial free city

▨ To Hapsburgs of Spain   ▨ To Brandenburg
▨ To Hapsburgs of Austria ▨ To Sweden
——— Boundary of Holy Roman Empire
✕ Battles

Baltic Sea

RÜGEN
HITHER POMERANIA
DUCHY OF MECKLENBURG-GÜSTROW
B. OF CAMMIN
FARTHER POMERANIA
Stettin
ATE OF BRANDENBURG
Berlin
Oder
Danzig
POMERELIA
ERMELAND
Königsberg
DUCHY OF PRUSSIA
(To Brandenburg 1618)

Thorn
Vistula
MAZOVIA
GREAT
KINGDOM
Posen
POLAND
Warsaw
OF
Kalisz
LITTLE
POLAND
POLAND

(To Brandenburg)
LUSATIA
✕ Breitenfeld
Leipzig
Lützen
E. OF SAXONY
Dresden
DUCHY
OF
Breslau
SILESIA
Cracow
GALICIA

White Mountain ✕ Prague
Elbe
KINGDOM
OF
BOHEMIA
Regensburg
MARGRAVIATE
OF
MORAVIA
TROPPAU
TESCHEN

B. OF PASSAU
ARCHDUCHY
Danube
OF Vienna
(To Freising)
Pressburg
HUNGARY

A/B OF SALZBURG
(To Freising)
AUSTRIA
(To Freising)
DUCHY
OF
STYRIA
KINGDOM OF
(To Austrian Hapsburgs)

(To Bamberg)
(To Salzburg)
(To Bamberg)
(To Salzburg)
(To Salzburg)
Freising)
(To Salzburg)
D. OF CARINTHIA
To Brixen)
(To Bamberg)
(To Brixen)
(To Freising)
C. OF GORIZIA
DUCHY
OF
CARNIOLA
Trieste
TURKISH HUNGARY

ICE
Adriatic Sea
Venice

A-451033-29-1-1-1-1 AL
Copyright by Rand McNally & Company, Made in U.S.A.

15°   20°

50°
45°

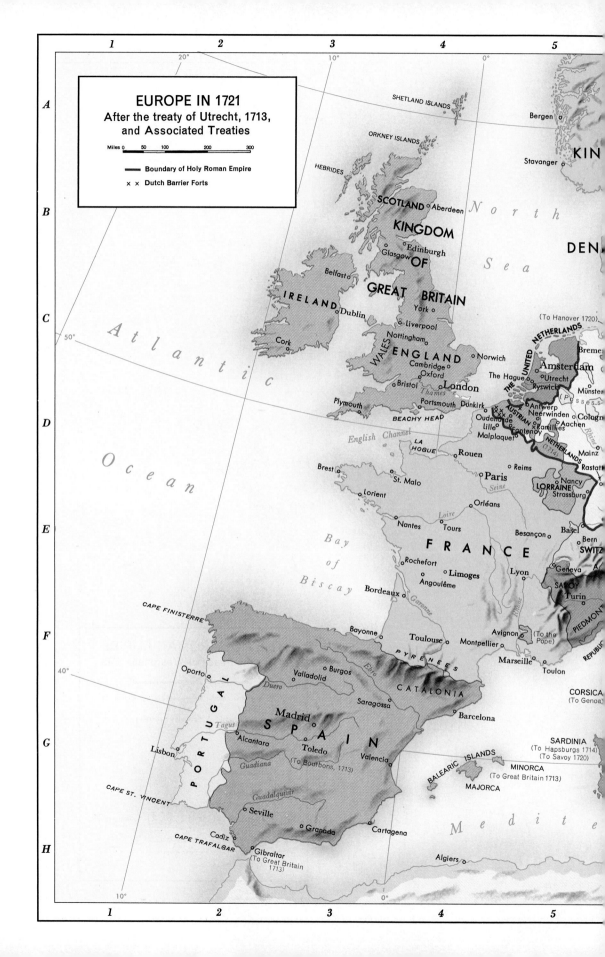

EUROPE IN 1721
After the treaty of Utrecht, 1713,
and Associated Treaties

Miles 0   50   100   200   300

—— Boundary of Holy Roman Empire
x x Dutch Barrier Forts

SHETLAND ISLANDS

ORKNEY ISLANDS

HEBRIDES

Bergen

Stavanger

KIN

DEN

North

Sea

SCOTLAND
Aberdeen

KINGDOM
Edinburgh
Glasgow
OF

Belfast

GREAT BRITAIN

IRELAND
Dublin
York

Liverpool

Nottingham

Cork

Norwich

(To Hanover 1720)

NETHERLANDS

Breme

WALES ENGLAND
Cambridge
Oxford
Bristol
London
Plymouth
Portsmouth Dunkirk
BEACHY HEAD

The Hague
Amsterdam
Utrecht
Ryswick
Münster

THE

AUSTRIAN

Antwerp
Oudenarde Neerwinden
Lille Ramillies
Malplaquet Fontenoy

Cologn
Aachen

Possess

English Channel
LA
HOGUE

NETHERLANDS
(1714)

Mainz

Rastat

Rouen

Brest
St. Malo

Reims
Paris
Seine

Nancy
LORRAINE
Strassburg

Atlantic

Ocean

Lorient

Orléans

Nantes
Tours

Loire

Besançon

Basel

Bern
SWITZ

Bay

of

Biscay

Rochefort
Limoges
Angoulême
Bordeaux
Garonne

FRANCE

Lyon

Geneva

Rhône

SA OY
Turin

PIEDMON

REPUBLI

Bayonne
Toulouse
Montpellier
PYRENEES

Avignon (To the
Pope)

Marseille
Toulon

CORSICA
(To Genoa)

CAPE FINISTERRE

Oporto

Burgos
Valladolid
Duero

Ebro

Saragossa

CATALONIA

Barcelona

Madrid

SARDINIA
(To Hapsburgs 1714)
(To Savoy 1720)

PORTUGAL

Tagus

SPAIN
Alcantara
Toledo

Valencia

BALEARIC ISLANDS
MINORCA
(To Great Britain 1713)

Lisbon

Guadiana

(To Bourbons, 1713)

MAJORCA

CAPE ST. VINCENT

Guadalquivir

Seville

Granada

Cartagena

Medite

Cadiz

CAPE TRAFALGAR

Gibraltar
(To Great Britain
1713)

Algiers

50°

40°

20°

10°

0°

10°

0°

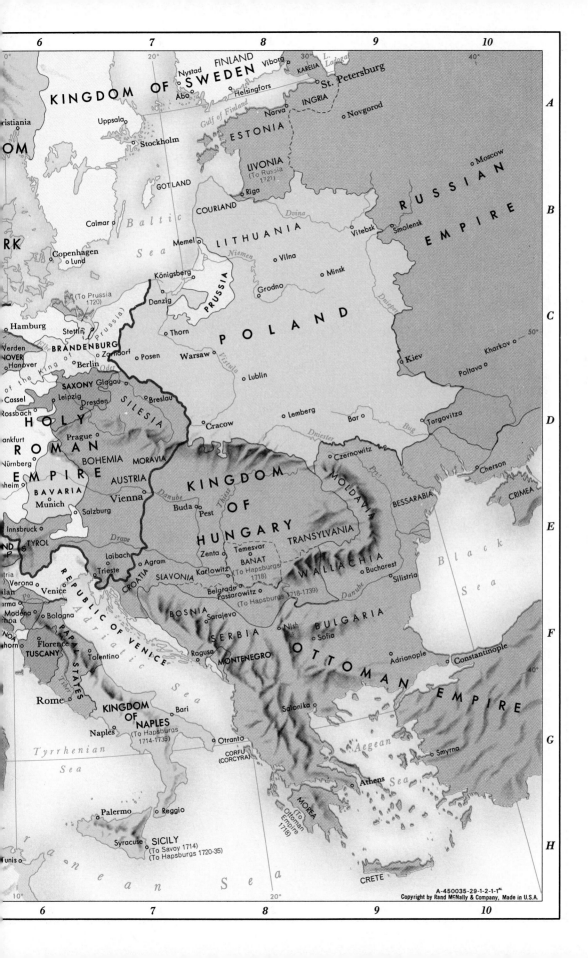

6   **7**   **8**   **9**   **10**

20°   FINLAND   30° L. Ladoga 40°

KINGDOM OF **SWEDEN**
Nystad Viborg KARELIA
Abo Helsingfors St. Petersburg
Gulf of Finland Narva INGRIA Novgorod **A**
Uppsala ESTONIA
Stockholm LIVONIA (To Russia 1721) Moscow
GOTLAND Riga
RUSSIAN EMPIRE

Calmar COURLAND Dvina Vitebsk Smolensk **B**
Baltic LITHUANIA
Copenhagen Memel Niemen Vilna
Lund Sea Minsk
Königsberg PRUSSIA Grodno Dnieper
(To Prussia 1720) Danzig POLAND **C**
Hamburg Stettin Thorn
Verden BRANDENBURG Zorndorf Posen Warsaw Kiev 50°
HANOVER Hanover Berlin Vistula Poltava
Cassel SAXONY Glogau Lublin
Rossbach Leipzig Dresden Breslau SILESIA
Frankfurt HOLY Prague Cracow Lemberg Bar Targovitza **D**
Nürnberg ROMAN BOHEMIA MORAVIA Dniester Bug
nheim EMPIRE AUSTRIA Czernowitz Cherson
BAVARIA Vienna KINGDOM MOLDAVIA CRIMEA
Munich Salzburg Danube Buda OF Theiss Pest BESSARABIA
Innsbruck TYROL HUNGARY **E**
Laibach Agram Zenta Temesvar TRANSYLVANIA Black
Verona Trieste CROATIA SLAVONIA Karlowitz BANAT (To Hapsburgs 1718) WALLACHIA Bucharest Sea
Venice REPUBLIC OF VENICE Belgrade Silistria
Milan Passarowitz (To Hapsburgs 1718-1739) Danube
Modena Bologna BOSNIA Sarajevo
Parma PAPAL STATES SERBIA Nish BULGARIA **F**
GENOA Florence TUSCANY Ragusa MONTENEGRO Sofia Adrianople Constantinople
horn Tolentino OTTOMAN EMPIRE 40°
Rome Tiber Bari Salonika
KINGDOM OF **NAPLES** (To Hapsburgs 1714-1735)
Naples Otranto Aegean **G**
Tyrrhenian CORFU (CORCYRA) Smyrna
Sea Athens Sea
Palermo Reggio MOREA (To Ottoman Empire 1718)
Syracuse **SICILY** (To Savoy 1714) (To Hapsburgs 1720-35) **H**
Tunis Sea CRETE
10° 20°

A-450035-29-1-2-1-1
Copyright by Rand McNally & Company, Made in U.S.A.

6   **7**   **8**   **9**   **10**

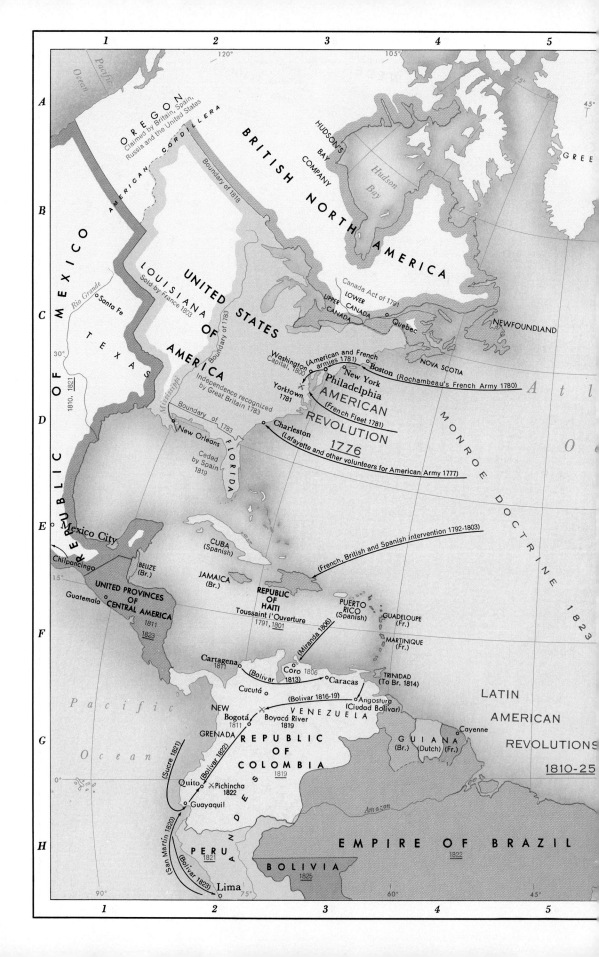

A

Pacific Ocean

OREGON
Claimed by Britain, Spain,
Russia and the United States

BRITISH NORTH AMERICA

AMERICAN CORDILLERA

Boundary of 1818

HUDSON'S BAY COMPANY

Hudson Bay

GREE

45°
60°

B

MEXICO

Rio Grande

LOUISIANA
OF
Sold by France 1803

UNITED
STATES
OF
AMERICA

Boundary of 1783

Canada Act of 1791

UPPER CANADA

LOWER CANADA

o Quebec

NEWFOUNDLAND

C

Santa Fe o

TEXAS

30°

1810, 1821

Mississippi

Independence recognized
by Great Britain 1783

Boundary of 1783

New Orleans

Washington
Capital, 1800

(American and French
armies 1781)

Yorktown
1781

Boston
(Rochambeau's French Army 1780)

New York

Philadelphia

AMERICAN
REVOLUTION
1776

(French Fleet 1781)

NOVA SCOTIA

Atl

D

FLORIDA

Ceded
by Spain
1819

Charleston

(Lafayette and other volunteers for American Army 1777)

MONROE DOCTRINE

O

E

REPUBLIC OF

Mexico City

Chilpancingo

BELIZE
(Br.)

CUBA
(Spanish)

JAMAICA
(Br.)

REPUBLIC
OF
HAITI
Toussaint l'Ouverture
1791, 1801

PUERTO
RICO
(Spanish)

(French, British and Spanish intervention 1792-1803)

GUADELOUPE
(Fr.)

1823

15°

F

UNITED PROVINCES
OF
CENTRAL AMERICA
Guatemala o

1811

1823

Pacific

Cartagena
1811

(Bolivar
1813)

Coro 1806

Caracas

(Miranda 1806)

MARTINIQUE
(Fr.)

TRINIDAD
(To Br. 1814)

LATIN

AMERICAN

G

Ocean

Cucutá o

NEW

GRENADA

Bogotá
1811

(Bolivar 1821)

(Bolivar 1822)

REPUBLIC
OF
COLOMBIA
1819

(Bolivar 1816-19)

VENEZUELA

Boyacá River
1819

Angostura
(Ciudad Bolivar)

GUIANA
(Br.) (Dutch) (Fr.)

Cayenne

REVOLUTIONS

1810-25

0°

H

(Sucre 1821)

Quito o

Guayaquil

(San Martín 1820)

x Pichincha
1822

Amazon

EMPIRE OF BRAZIL
1822

PERU
1821

(Bolivar 1823)

BOLIVIA
1825

Lima

90°

75°

60°

45°

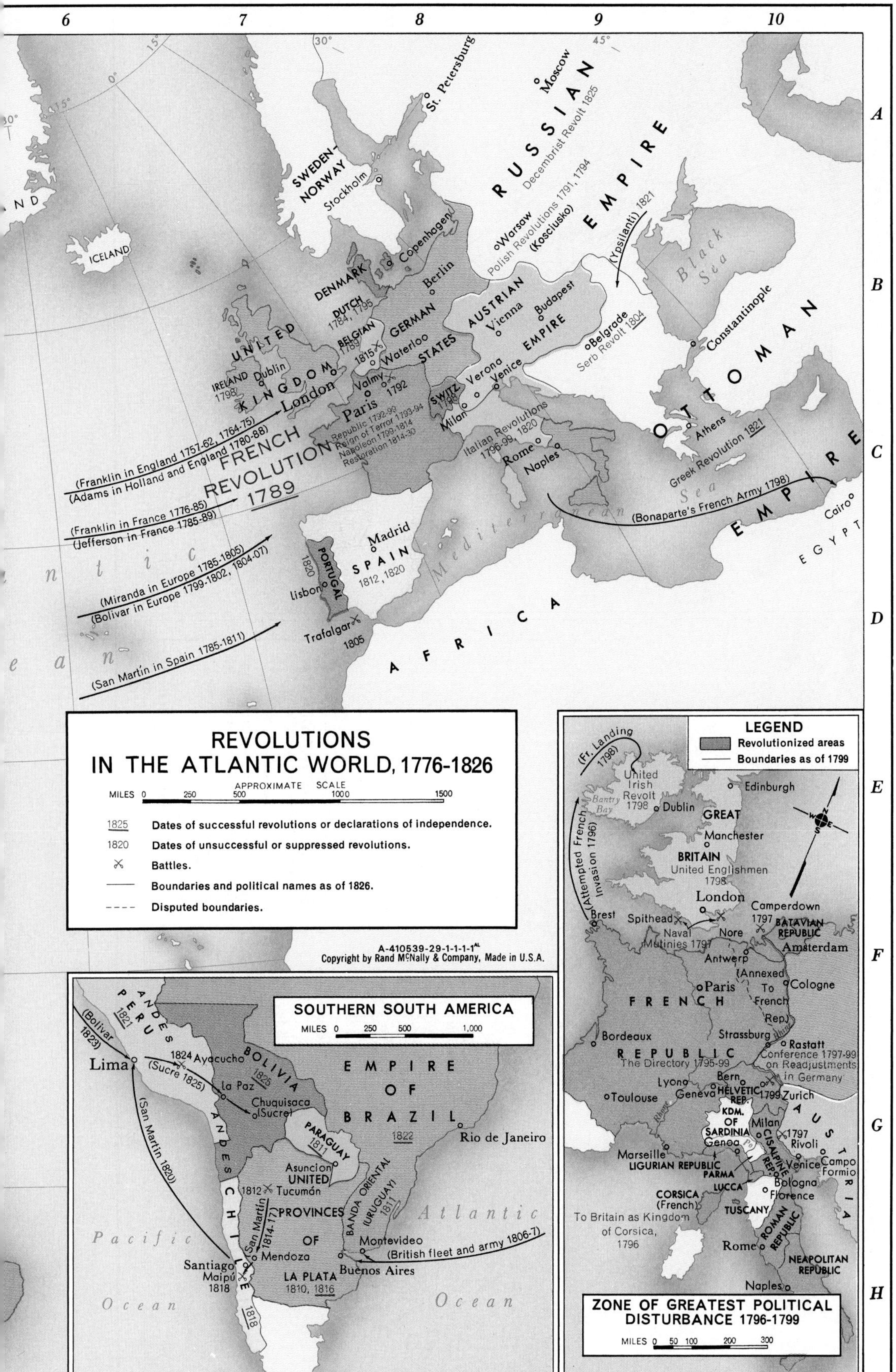
REVOLUTIONS IN THE ATLANTIC WORLD, 1776-1826
MILES 0 250 500 1000 1500
APPROXIMATE SCALE
1825 Dates of successful revolutions or declarations of independence.
1820 Dates of unsuccessful or suppressed revolutions.
Battles.
Boundaries and political names as of 1826.
Disputed boundaries.
A-410539-29-1-1-1-1
Copyright by Rand McNally & Company, Made in U.S.A.
RUSSIAN EMPIRE
Decembrist Revolt 1825
Moscow
St. Petersburg
SWEDEN-NORWAY
Stockholm
Warsaw
Polish Revolutions 1791, 1794 (Kosciusko)
(Ypsilanti) 1821
ICELAND
DENMARK
Copenhagen
Berlin
DUTCH 1784, 1795
BELGIAN 1789
GERMAN STATES
Waterloo 1815
AUSTRIAN EMPIRE
Vienna
Budapest
Belgrade
Serb Revolt 1804
Constantinople
OTTOMAN EMPIRE
Black Sea
UNITED KINGDOM
IRELAND 1798
Dublin
London
Valmy 1792
Paris
Republic 1792-99
Reign of Terror 1793-94
Napoleon 1799-1814
Restoration 1814-30
SWITZ. 1798
Verona
Venice
Milan
Italian Revolutions 1796-99, 1820
Rome
Naples
Athens
Greek Revolution 1821
(Bonaparte's French Army 1798)
Cairo
EGYPT
Mediterranean Sea
FRENCH REVOLUTION 1789
(Franklin in England 1757-62, 1764-75)
(Adams in Holland and England 1780-88)
(Franklin in France 1776-85)
(Jefferson in France 1785-89)
(Miranda in Europe 1785-1805)
(Bolivar in Europe 1799-1802, 1804-07)
(San Martín in Spain 1785-1811)
Atlantic Ocean
PORTUGAL 1820
Lisbon
Madrid
SPAIN 1812, 1820
Trafalgar 1805
AFRICA
SOUTHERN SOUTH AMERICA
MILES 0 250 500 1,000
PERU 1821
(Bolivar 1823)
Lima
1824 Ayacucho
(Sucre 1825)
La Paz
BOLIVIA 1825
Chuquisaca (Sucre)
ANDES
EMPIRE OF BRAZIL 1822
Rio de Janeiro
PARAGUAY 1811
Asuncion
(San Martín 1820)
1812 Tucumán
UNITED PROVINCES OF LA PLATA 1810, 1816
BANDA ORIENTAL (URUGUAY) 1811
San Martín 1814-17
Mendoza
Montevideo
Buenos Aires
(British fleet and army 1806-7)
CHILE 1818
Santiago
Maipú 1818
Pacific Ocean
Atlantic Ocean
LEGEND
Revolutionized areas
Boundaries as of 1799
(Fr. Landing 1798)
United Irish Revolt 1798
Bantry Bay
Dublin
Edinburgh
GREAT BRITAIN
Manchester
United Englishmen 1798
London
(Attempted French Invasion 1796)
Brest
Spithead
Naval Mutinies 1797
Nore
Camperdown 1797
BATAVIAN REPUBLIC
Amsterdam
Antwerp
(Annexed To French Rep.)
Cologne
Paris
FRENCH REPUBLIC
The Directory 1795-99
Bordeaux
Strassburg
Rastatt Conference 1797-99 on Readjustments in Germany
Bern
HELVETIC REP.
1799 Zurich
Lyon
Geneva
Toulouse
KDM. OF SARDINIA
Genoa
Milan
CISALPINE REP.
1797 Rivoli
AUSTRIA
Venice
Campo Formio
Marseille
LIGURIAN REPUBLIC
PARMA
LUCCA
Bologna
Florence
CORSICA (French)
TUSCANY
To Britain as Kingdom of Corsica, 1796
ROMAN REPUBLIC
Rome
NEAPOLITAN REPUBLIC
Naples
ZONE OF GREATEST POLITICAL DISTURBANCE 1796-1799
MILES 0 50 100 200 300

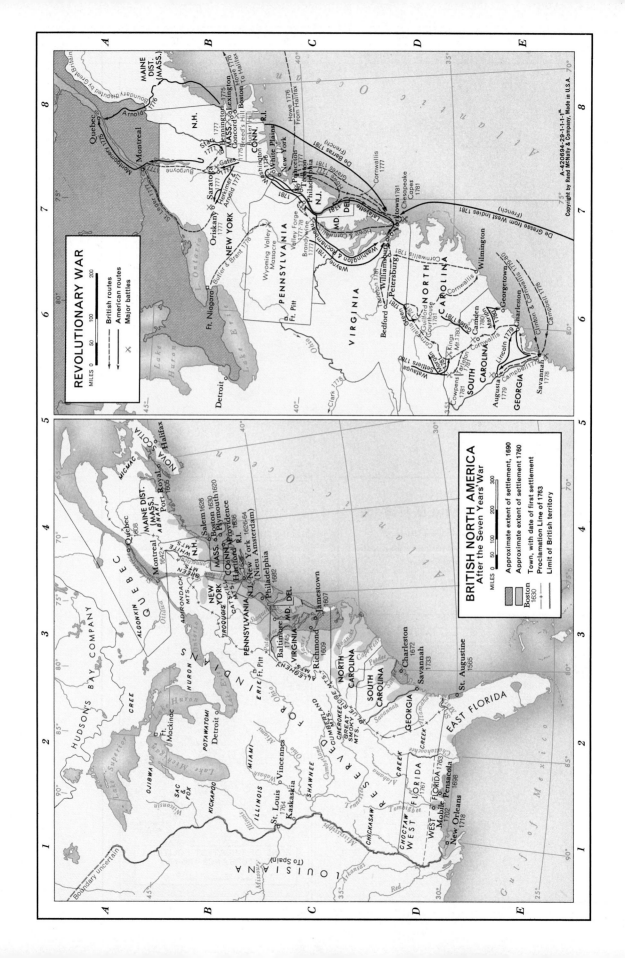

REVOLUTIONARY WAR

MILES
0   50 100 200

— British routes
→ American routes
✕ Major battles

QUEBEC

Montgomery 1775
Quebec 1775
Arnold 1776
Montreal

Boundary disputed by Great Britain

MAINE DIST. (MASS.)

N.H.

Stark 1777
Bennington 1775
Lexington 1775
Concord 1775
Breed's Hill
Bunker Hill
Boston 1776
Howe 1776 To Halifax

CONN.
R.I.

Howe 1776 From Halifax

White Plains 1776
New York

Saratoga 1777
Gates 1777
Herkimer
Arnold 1777

Oriskany 1777 ✕

NEW YORK

Burgoyne 1777

St. Lawrence

De Barras 1781
Graves 1781

Ft. Niagara
Butler & Brant 1778

L. Ontario

Wyoming Valley Massacre

PENNSYLVANIA

Ft. Pitt

Valley Forge 1777-78
Brandywine 1777

Washington 1776
Princeton 1777
Trenton 1777
Philadelphia
N.J.

Wayne 1781

MD.
DEL.

Washington & Rochambeau 1781
Howe & Cornwallis

Lafayette 1781

Cornwallis 1777

Yorktown 1781
Chesapeake Capes 1781

De Grasse from West Indies 1781 (French)

Detroit

L. Huron

L. Erie

Ohio

Clark 1778

VIRGINIA

Bedford
Williamsburg
Petersburg
Cornwallis 1781

Greene 1781
Guilford Courthouse 1781

NORTH CAROLINA

Cornwallis

Wilmington
Cornwallis 1781

Gates 1780
Kings Mtn. 1780

Watauga Settlers 1780

Cowpens 1781
Tarleton 1781

Camden 1780
Marion

Georgetown 1780

SOUTH CAROLINA

Lincoln 1779
Cornwallis

Charleston
Clinton & Cornwallis 1780
Campbell 1779

Augusta 1779

GEORGIA

Savannah 1778
Campbell 1778

A-420694-29-1-1-1^AL
Copyright by Rand McNally & Company, Made in U.S.A.

BRITISH NORTH AMERICA
After the Seven Years' War

MILES
0 50 100 200   300

Approximate extent of settlement, 1690
Approximate extent of settlement, 1760

Boston
1630   Town, with date of first settlement

— + — Proclamation Line of 1763
—·—   Limit of British territory

HUDSON'S BAY COMPANY

CREE

MICMAC

NOVA SCOTIA

Port Royal 1605
Halifax

QUEBEC

Quebec 1608

Montreal 1642

ALGONKIN INDIANS

ADIRONDACK MTS.

WHITE MTS.
MAINE DIST. (MASS.)
ABNAKI

N.H.

GREEN MTS.

Salem 1626
MASS. Boston 1630
Plymouth 1620
Providence
CONN. 1636
Hartford 1635 R.I.

NEW YORK
IROQUOIS
New York 1626-64 (Nieu Amsterdam)

CATSKILL MTS.

OJIBWA

POTAWATOMI

Ft. Mackinac

Detroit

MIAMI

ILLINOIS

SAC & FOX

KICKAPOO

Lake Superior

Lake Michigan

Lake Huron

HURON

ERIE

OTTAWA

SHAWNEE

St. Louis 1764
Kaskaskia

Vincennes

ALLEGHENY MTS.

Ft. Pitt

PENNSYLVANIA

Philadelphia 1682

MD.
DEL.

Baltimore 1745

Richmond 1609
VIRGINIA
Jamestown 1607

CUMBERLAND MTS.
GREAT SMOKY MTS.
CHEROKEE
BLUE RIDGE MTS.

NORTH CAROLINA

Charleston 1672

SOUTH CAROLINA

Savannah 1733

GEORGIA

CREEK

CHICKASAW

CHOCTAW

WEST FLORIDA
1763
1767

Mobile 1702
Pensacola 1698

New Orleans 1718

EAST FLORIDA

St. Augustine 1565

LOUISIANA (To Spain)

Boundary uncertain

Gulf of Mexico

A T L A N T I C   O C E A N

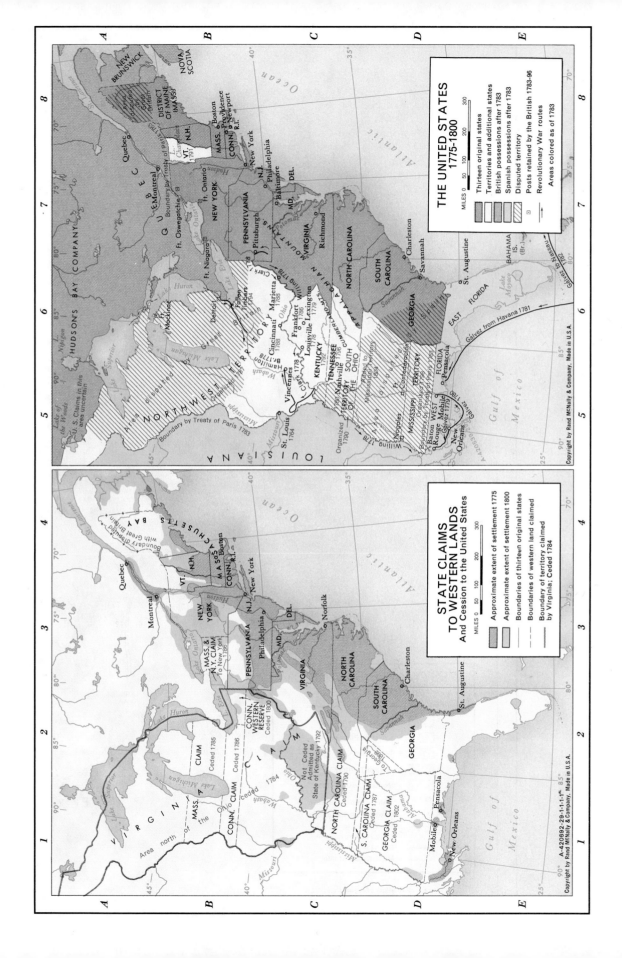

THE UNITED STATES
1775-1800

MILES 0 50 100 200 300

- Thirteen original states
- Territories and additional states
- British possessions after 1783
- Spanish possessions after 1783
- Disputed territory
- ⊡ Posts retained by the British 1783-96
- → Revolutionary War routes
- Areas colored as of 1783

Copyright by Rand McNally & Company. Made in U.S.A.

STATE CLAIMS
TO WESTERN LANDS
And Cession to the United States

MILES 0 50 100 200 300

- Approximate extent of settlement 1775
- Approximate extent of settlement 1800
- Boundaries of thirteen original states
- Boundaries of western land claimed
- Boundary of territory claimed by Virginia; Ceded 1784

A-420692-29-1-1-1¼ AL. Made in U.S.A.
Copyright by Rand McNally & Company. Made in U.S.A.

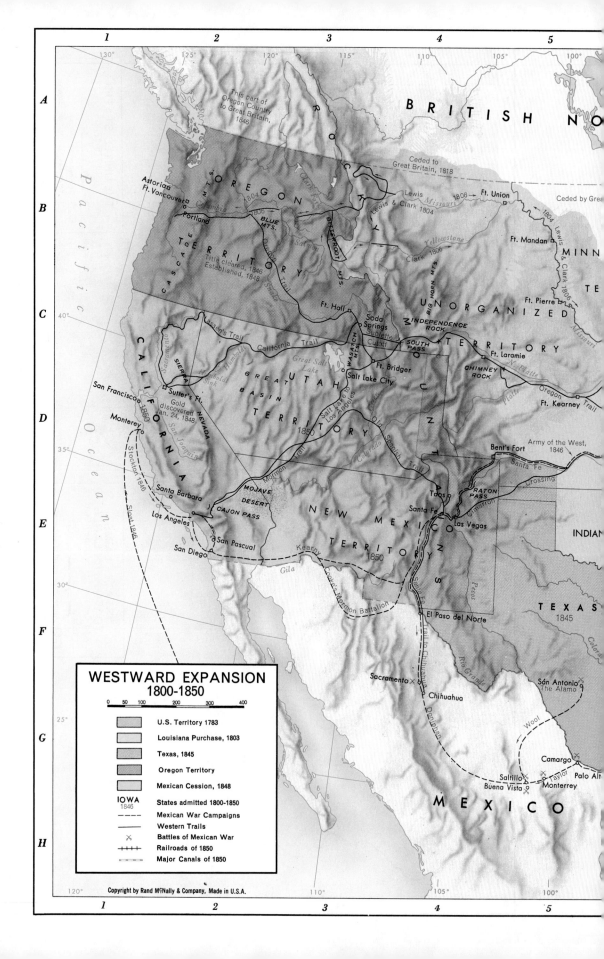

WESTWARD EXPANSION
1800-1850

0 50 100   200   300   400

	U.S. Territory 1783
	Louisiana Purchase, 1803
	Texas, 1845
	Oregon Territory
	Mexican Cession, 1848
IOWA 1846	States admitted 1800-1850
– – –	Mexican War Campaigns
———	Western Trails
×	Battles of Mexican War
+++++	Railroads of 1850
▭–▭	Major Canals of 1850

Copyright by Rand McNally & Company, Made in U.S.A.

34

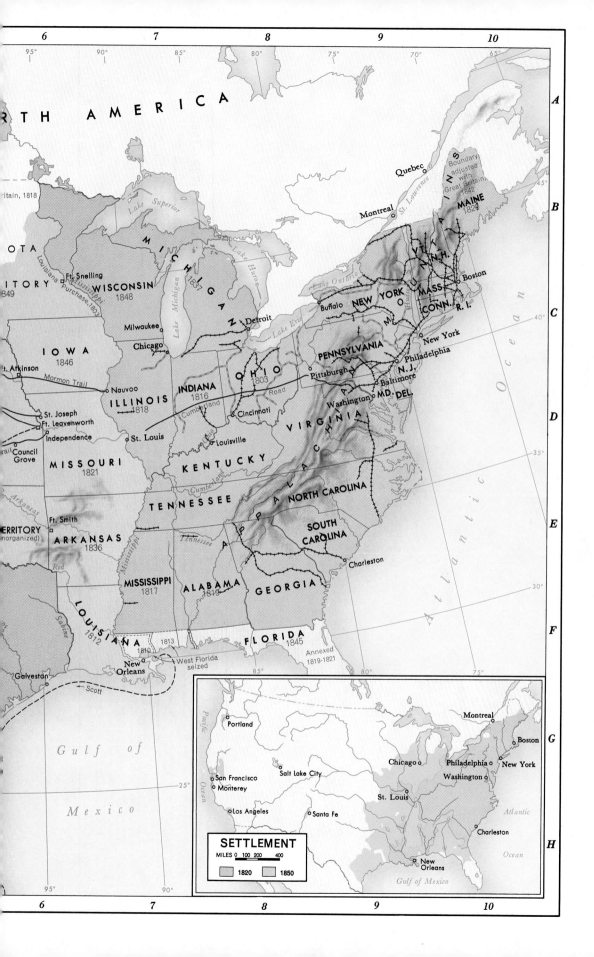

NORTH AMERICA

Quebec

Montreal

St. Lawrence

Boundary
adjusted
with
Great Britain
1842

MAINE
1820

Britain, 1818

Lake Superior

Ft. Snelling

Louisiana Purchase, 1803

Mississippi

MINNESOTA

TERRITORY
1849

WISCONSIN
1848

MICHIGAN
1837

Lake Michigan

Lake Huron

Milwaukee

Detroit

Lake Erie

Lake Ontario

Buffalo

NEW YORK

VT.
N.H.
MASS.
CONN.
R.I.

Boston

New York

Chicago

IOWA
1846

Ft. Atkinson

Mormon Trail

Nauvoo

ILLINOIS
1818

INDIANA
1816

OHIO
1803

Cumberland Road

PENNSYLVANIA

N.J.

Philadelphia

Pittsburgh

Baltimore

St. Joseph

Ft. Leavenworth

Independence

St. Louis

Louisville

Cincinnati

Washington
MD.
DEL.

VIRGINIA

APPALACHIANS

Council
Grove

MISSOURI
1821

KENTUCKY

TENNESSEE

Cumberland

Tennessee

NORTH CAROLINA

SOUTH
CAROLINA

Arkansas

INDIAN TERRITORY
(unorganized)

Ft. Smith

ARKANSAS
1836

Red

MISSISSIPPI
1817

ALABAMA
1819

GEORGIA

Charleston

Atlantic Ocean

40°

45°

35°

30°

LOUISIANA
1812

1813

1810

West Florida
seized

FLORIDA
1845

Annexed
1819-1821

Sabine

Galveston

New
Orleans

Scott

Gulf   of

Mexico

85°

80°

75°

A

B

C

D

E

F

Portland

Montreal

Boston

Pacific
Ocean

Salt Lake City

Chicago

Philadelphia

New York

San Francisco
Monterey

St. Louis

Washington

Los Angeles

Santa Fe

Charleston

Atlantic
Ocean

New
Orleans

Gulf of Mexico

G

H

SETTLEMENT

MILES 0 100 200   400

1820   1850

95°   90°   85°   80°

6   7   8   9   10

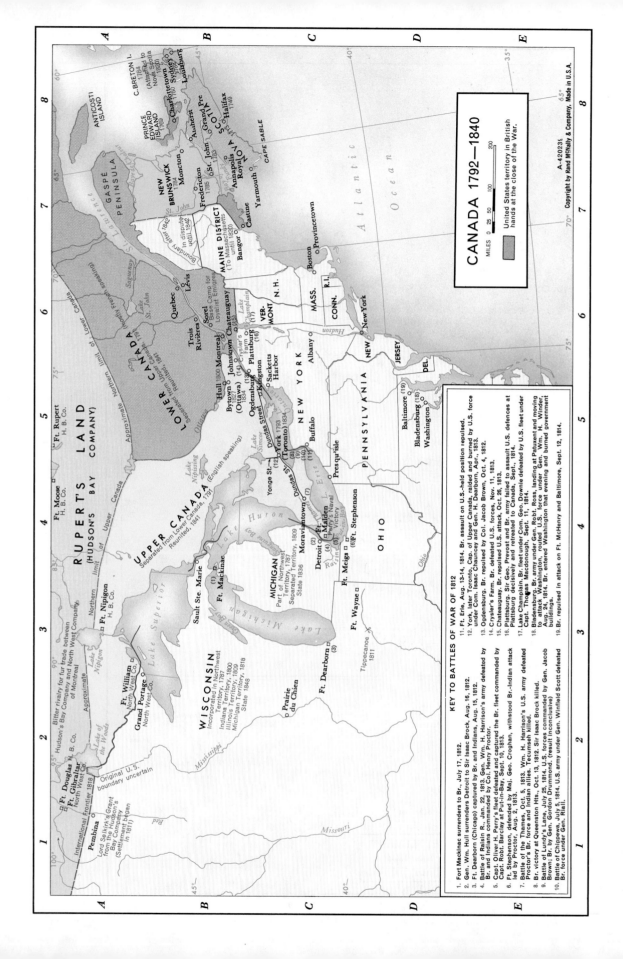

CANADA 1792—1840

MILES 0 25 50 100 200

☐ United States territory in British hands at the close of the War.

Copyright by Rand McNally & Company, Made in U.S.A.

A-42023i

KEY TO BATTLES OF WAR OF 1812

1. Fort Mackinac surrenders to Br., July 17, 1812.
2. Gen. Wm. Hull surrenders Detroit to Sir Isaac Brock, Aug. 16, 1812.
3. Ft. Dearborn (Chicago) captured by Br. and Indians, Aug. 15, 1812.
4. Battle of Raisin R., Jan. 22, 1813. Gen. Wm. H. Harrison's army defeated by Br. and Indians commanded by Col. Henry Proctor.
5. Capt. Oliver H. Perry's fleet defeated and captured the Br. fleet commanded by Capt. Robt. Barclay at Put-in-Bay, Sept. 10, 1813.
6. Ft. Stephenson, defended by Maj. Geo. Croghan, withstood Br.-Indian attack led by Proctor, Aug. 2, 1813.
7. Battle of the Thames, Oct. 5, 1813. Wm. H. Harrison's U.S. army defeated Proctor's Br. force and Indian allies. Tecumseh killed.
8. Br. victory at Queenston Hts., Oct. 13, 1812. Sir Isaac Brock killed.
9. Battle of Lundy's Lane, July 25, 1814. U.S. forces commanded by Gen. Jacob Brown; Br. by Gen. Gordon Drummond. (result inconclusive)
10. Battle of Chippewa, July 5, 1814. U.S. army under Gen. Winfield Scott defeated Br. force under Gen. Riall.
11. Ft. Erie, Aug. 13-14, 1814. Br. assault on U.S.-held position repulsed.
12. York, later Toronto, Cap. of Upper Canada, raided and burned by U.S. force under Com. Isaac Chauncey and Gen. H. Dearborn, Apr., 1813.
13. Ogdensburg. Br. repulsed by Col. Jacob Brown, Oct. 4, 1812.
14. Crysler's Farm. Br. defeated U.S. forces, Nov. 11, 1813.
15. Chateauguay, Br. repulsed U.S. attack, Oct. 26, 1813.
16. Plattsburg. Sir Geo. Prevost and Br. army failed to assault U.S. defences at Plattsburg decisively and retreated to Canada, Sept., 1814.
17. Lake Champlain, Br. fleet under Com. Geo. Downie defeated by U.S. fleet under Capt. Thomas Macdonough, Sept. 11, 1814.
18. Bladensburg. Br. army under Gen. Robt. Ross, landing at Patuxent and moving to attack Washington, routed U.S. force under Gen. Wm. H. Winder, Aug. 24, 1814. Br. entered Washington that evening and burned government buildings.
19. Br. repulsed in attack on Ft. McHenry and Baltimore, Sept. 12, 1814.

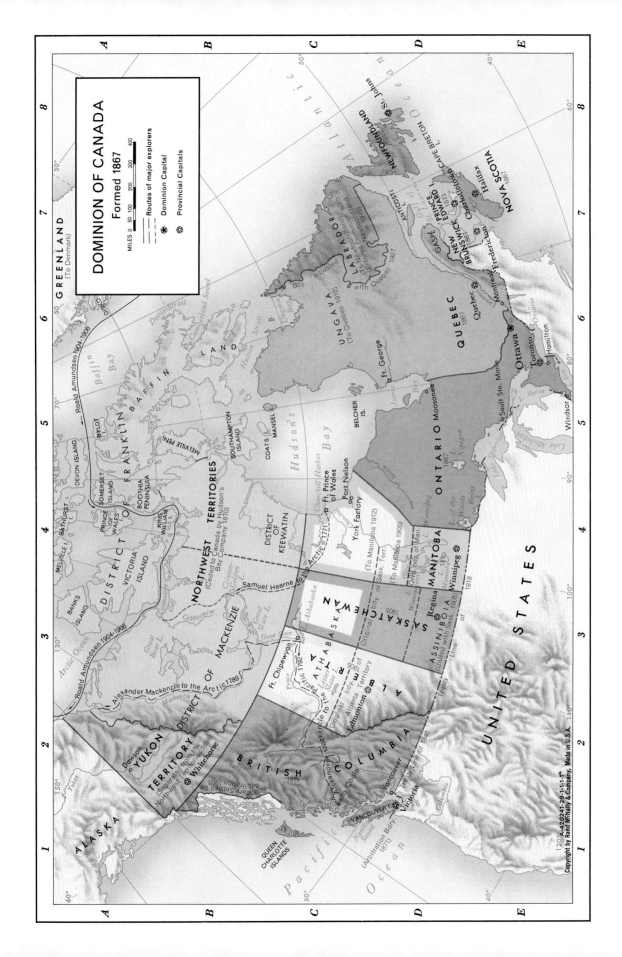

DOMINION OF CANADA
Formed 1867

MILES 0 50 100 200 300 400

⊕ Routes of major explorers
⊛ Dominion Capital
⊗ Provincial Capitals

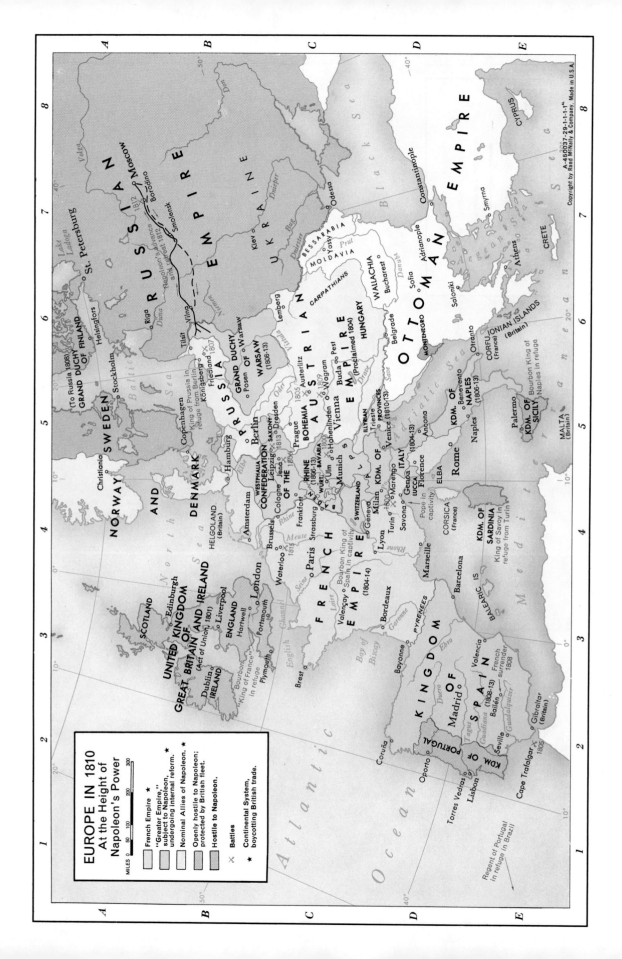

EUROPE IN 1810
At the Height of Napoleon's Power

MILES 0 50 100 200 300

French Empire ★

"Greater Empire," subject to Napoleon, undergoing internal reform. ★

Nominal Allies of Napoleon. ★

Openly hostile to Napoleon; protected by British fleet.

Hostile to Napoleon.

Battles ⚔

Continental System, boycotting British trade. ★

38

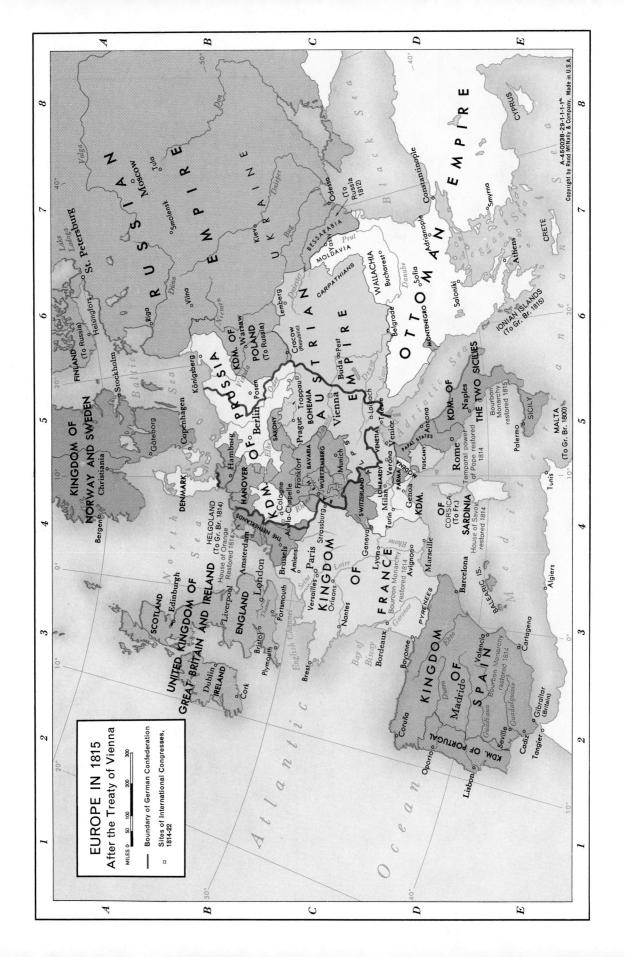

EUROPE IN 1815
After the Treaty of Vienna

MILES 0 50 100 200 300

—— Boundary of German Confederation

▫ Sites of International Congresses, 1814-22

RUSSIAN EMPIRE

Volga
Don
Moscow
Tula
St. Petersburg
Lake Ladoga
Helsingfors
FINLAND (To Russia)
Riga
Vilna
Smolensk
Dvina
Kiev
UKRAINE
Dnieper
Bug
Dniester
Lemberg
Odessa
(To Russia 1812)

KINGDOM OF NORWAY AND SWEDEN
Bergen
Christiania
Göteborg
Stockholm
Baltic Sea
Copenhagen
DENMARK
Königsberg
KDM. OF POLAND (To Russia)
Warsaw
Posen
Vistula
Oder
Cracow (Republic)

KDM. OF PRUSSIA
Berlin
Hamburg
Elbe
SAXONY
Prague
BOHEMIA
Troppau
Brünn

HANOVER KDM. OF
Cologne
Aix-la-Chapelle
Frankfort
BAVARIA
Munich
WÜRTEMBERG
Strassburg
SWITZERLAND
Geneva

THE NETHERLANDS
House of Orange Restored 1814
Amsterdam
Brussels

UNITED KINGDOM OF GREAT BRITAIN AND IRELAND
SCOTLAND
Edinburgh
ENGLAND
London
Liverpool
Bristol
Portsmouth
Plymouth
IRELAND
Dublin
Cork
North Sea
HELGOLAND (To Gr. Br. 1814)
English Channel

KINGDOM OF FRANCE
Bourbon Monarchy restored 1814
Paris
Versailles
Amiens
Orléans
Nantes
Brest
Bordeaux
Bayonne
Lyon
Marseille
Avignon
Seine
Loire
Garonne
Rhone
PYRENEES
Bay of Biscay
Atlantic Ocean

AUSTRIAN EMPIRE
Vienna
Buda
Pest
Drave
Save
Laibach
Trieste
Carpathians

KINGDOM OF SPAIN
Bourbon Monarchy restored 1814
Madrid
Valencia
Coruña
Barcelona
Seville
Cadiz
Gibraltar (Britain)
Cartagena
Duero
Tagus
Guadiana
Guadalquivir
Ebro
BALEARIC IS.
Tangier
Algiers

KDM. OF PORTUGAL
Oporto
Lisbon

LOMBARDY
Milan
Turin
Genoa
VENETIA
Verona
Venice
Adige
Po
SARDINIA KDM.
House of Savoy restored 1814
CORSICA (To Fr.)
PARMA
MODENA
TUSCANY
PAPAL STATES
Ancona
Rome
Temporal power of Pope restored 1814

KDM. OF THE TWO SICILIES
Bourbon Monarchy restored 1815
Naples
SICILY
Palermo
MALTA (To Gr. Br. 1800)
Tunis
Mediterranean Sea
Adriatic Sea

OTTOMAN EMPIRE
Belgrade
MONTENEGRO
Sofia
Danube
WALLACHIA
Bucharest
MOLDAVIA
BESSARABIA
Prut
Constantinople
Adrianople
Salonki
Athens
Smyrna
Black Sea
Aegean Sea
IONIAN ISLANDS (To Gr. Br. 1815)
CRETE
CYPRUS

A-450038-29-1-1-1ᴬᴬ
Copyright by Rand McNally & Company. Made in U.S.A.

39

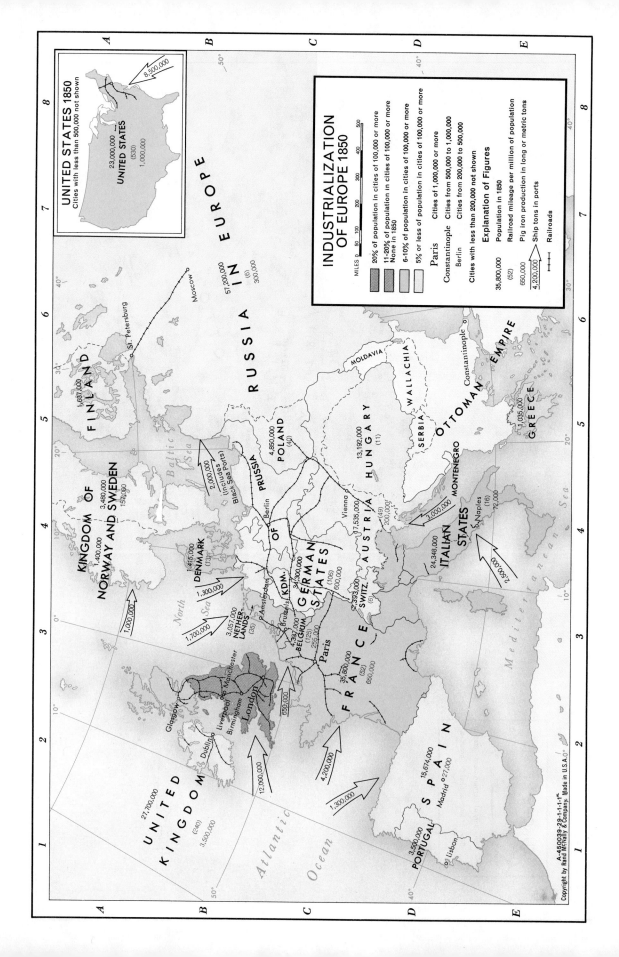

UNITED STATES 1850
Cities with less than 500,000 not shown

UNITED STATES
(530)
1,000,000

23,000,000
8,500,000

INDUSTRIALIZATION OF EUROPE 1850

MILES 0 50 100 200 300 400 500

20% of population in cities of 100,000 or more
11-20% of population in cities of 100,000 or more
None in 1850
6-10% of population in cities of 100,000 or more
5% or less of population in cities of 100,000 or more

Paris   Cities of 1,000,000 or more
Constantinople Cities from 500,000 to 1,000,000
Berlin   Cities from 200,000 to 500,000
Cities with less than 200,000 not shown

Explanation of Figures

35,800,000   Population in 1850

(52)   Railroad mileage per million of population

650,000   Pig iron production in long or metric tons

4,200,000   Ship tons in ports

Railroads

EUROPE

RUSSIA IN

Moscow
57,200,000
(6)
300,000

St. Petersburg
1,637,000

FINLAND

KINGDOM OF
NORWAY AND SWEDEN
1,400,000
3,480,000
150,000

Baltic Sea

2,000,000
(includes Black Sea Ports)

PRUSSIA

POLAND
4,850,000
(40)

Berlin

OF

Vienna
17,535,000
(49)
200,000

AUSTRIA HUNGARY
13,192,000
(11)

MOLDAVIA

WALLACHIA

SERBIA

MONTENEGRO

OTTOMAN EMPIRE

Constantinople

GREECE
1,035,000

North Sea

DENMARK
1,415,000
(13)
1,300,000

1,700,000

Amsterdam
NETHER-
LANDS
3,057,000
(35)

Brussels
BELGIUM
4,337,000
(125)
255,000

KDM.

GERMAN
STATES
34,300,000
(106)
600,000

SWITZ.
2,393,000
(6)

ITALIAN
STATES
24,348,000
(16)

3,000,000

Naples
2,000
2,500,000

1,000,000

12,000,000

Glasgow
Dublin
Liverpool Manchester
London
Birmingham

UNITED
KINGDOM
27,700,000
(240)
3,500,000

Atlantic Ocean

650,000

Paris
35,600,000
(52)
660,000

FRANCE

4,200,000

1,300,000

SPAIN
15,674,000
Madrid 27,000

PORTUGAL
3,500,000
Lisbon

Mediterranean Sea

A-450039-29-1-1-1-1
Copyright by Rand McNally & Company. Made in U.S.A.

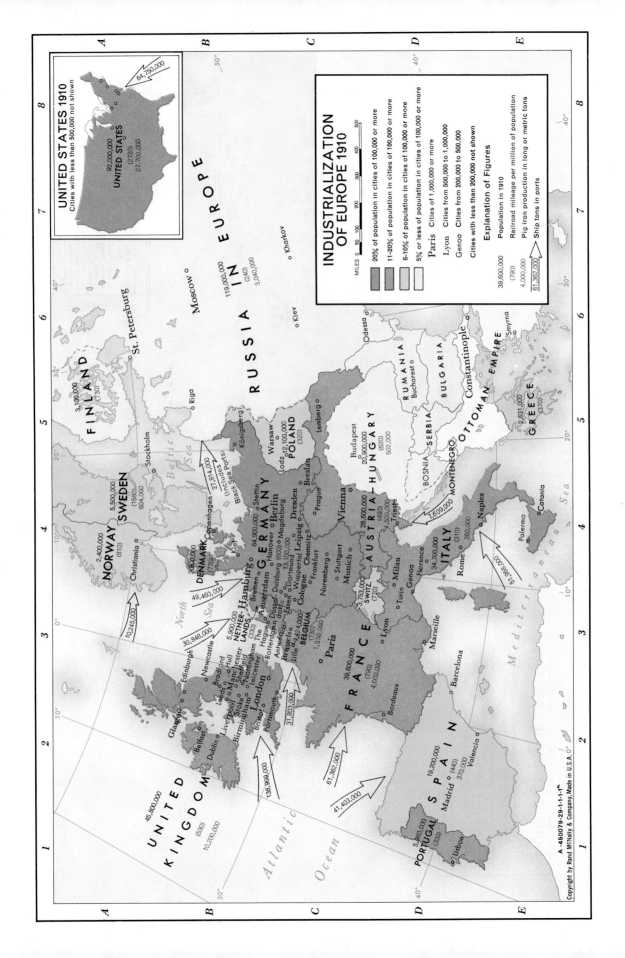

INDUSTRIALIZATION OF EUROPE 1910

MILES 0 50 100 200 300 400 500

- 20% of population in cities of 100,000 or more
- 11–20% of population in cities of 100,000 or more
- 6–10% of population in cities of 100,000 or more
- 5% or less of population in cities of 100,000 or more
- Cities with less than 200,000 not shown

Paris Cities of 1,000,000 or more
Lyon Cities from 500,000 to 1,000,000
Genoa Cities from 200,000 to 500,000
Cities with less than 200,000 not shown

Explanation of Figures

39,600,000 Population in 1910
(790) Railroad mileage per million of population
4,000,000 Pig iron production in long or metric tons
61,362,000 Ship tons in ports

UNITED STATES 1910
Cities with less than 500,000 not shown

UNITED STATES
92,000,000
(2720)
27,700,000

64,750,000

EUROPE

FINLAND
3,100,000
(730)

NORWAY
2,400,000
(810)
Christiania

SWEDEN
5,500,000
(1580)
604,000
Stockholm

RUSSIA
119,000,000
(240)
3,040,000

St. Petersburg
Moscow
Riga
Kharkov
Kiev
Odessa

DENMARK
2,800,000
(770)
Copenhagen

27,814,000
(Includes Black Sea Ports)
Königsberg

GERMANY
64,900,000
(600)
13,100,000

Kiel
Hamburg
Bremen
Hanover
Berlin
Magdeburg
Dresden
Leipzig
Chemnitz
Prague
Breslau
Warsaw
Lodz 12,100,000
POLAND
(320)
Lemberg

49,460,000

NETHER-
LANDS
5,900,000
(330)
Amsterdam
The Hague
Rotterdam
Antwerp

BELGIUM
7,424,000
(730)
1,330,000
Brussels
Lille

Dortmund
Essen
Düsseldorf
Duisburg
Wupperal
Cologne
Frankfurt
Nuremberg
Stuttgart
Munich

SWITZ.
3,753,000
(770)

AUSTRIA-HUNGARY
28,600,000
(490)
1,500,000
Vienna
Budapest
20,900,000
(620)
502,000
Trieste

1,609,000
MONTENEGRO
BOSNIA
SERBIA
RUMANIA
Bucharest
BULGARIA
Constantinople
OTTOMAN EMPIRE

GREECE
2,631,000
(370)
Smyrna

30,848,000

UNITED KINGDOM
45,800,000
(630)
10,200,000

Glasgow
Edinburgh
Belfast
Newcastle
Dublin
Liverpool
Leeds
Bradford
Hull
Manchester
Sheffield
Stoke
Nottingham
Birmingham
Leicester
London 31,803,900
Bristol
Portsmouth

138,909,000

FRANCE
39,600,000
(790)
4,000,000

Paris
Lyon
Bordeaux
Marseille

61,362,000

41,403,000

PORTUGAL
5,960,000
(330)
Lisbon

SPAIN
19,200,000
(440)
370,000
Madrid
Valencia
Barcelona

ITALY
34,700,000
(310)
360,000
Rome
Milan
Turin
Genoa
Florence
Naples
Palermo
Catania

51,998,000

Atlantic Ocean
North Sea
Baltic Sea
Mediterranean Sea

A -450079-29-1-1-1-1™
Copyright by Rand McNally & Company, Made in U.S.A.

41

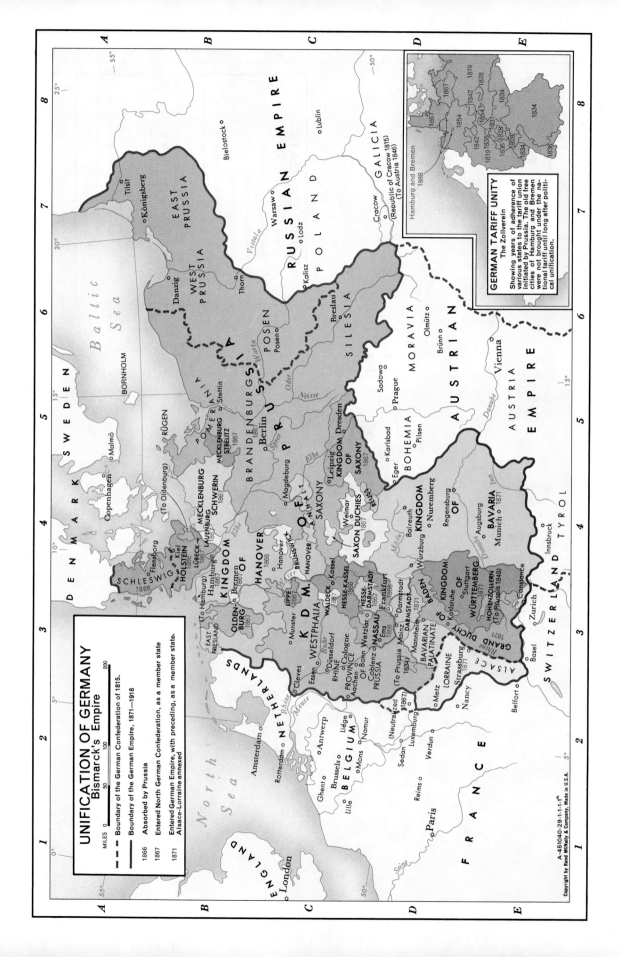

UNIFICATION OF GERMANY
Bismarck's Empire

MILES 0   50   100   200

- - -   Boundary of the German Confederation of 1815.
———   Boundary of the German Empire, 1871—1918
         Absorbed by Prussia
1866   Entered North German Confederation, as a member state
1867   Entered German Empire, with preceding, as a member state.
1871   Alsace-Lorraine annexed

GERMAN TARIFF UNITY
The Zollverein

Showing years of adherence of various states to the tariff union initiated by Prussia. The old free cities of Hamburg and Bremen were not brought under the national tariff until long after political unification.

A-451040-29-1-1-1-1-1 AL

Copyright by Rand McNally & Company, Made in U.S.A.

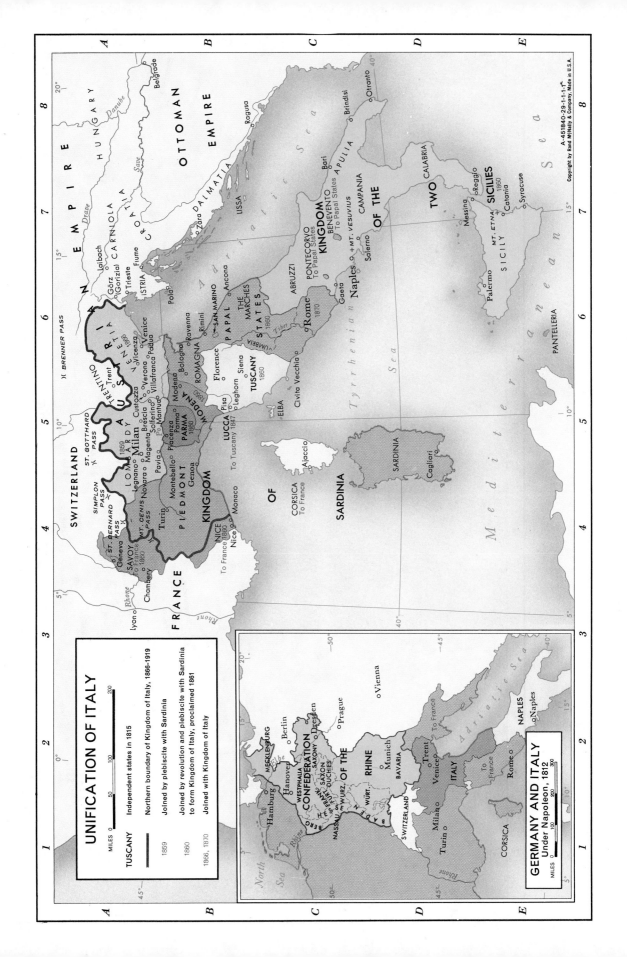

UNIFICATION OF ITALY

MILES
0   50   100   200

TUSCANY   Independent states in 1815

Northern boundary of Kingdom of Italy, 1866-1919

1859   Joined by plebiscite with Sardinia

1860   Joined by revolution and plebiscite with Sardinia to form Kingdom of Italy, proclaimed 1861

1866, 1870   Joined with Kingdom of Italy

GERMANY AND ITALY
Under Napoleon, 1812

MILES
0   100   200   300

SWITZERLAND

FRANCE

SAVOY
To France
1860

NICE
To France

PIEDMONT

KINGDOM

Turin

Genoa

Monaco
Nice

Geneva

Chambery

ST. BERNARD PASS

SIMPLON PASS

ST. GOTTHARD PASS

MT. CENIS PASS

BRENNER PASS

LOMBARDY

Milan
1859

Legnano
Novaro

Pavia

Montebello

Magenta

Brescia
Solferino
Custozza
Villafranca

Mantua

Piacenza

PARMA
1860
Parma
Modena

MODENA

LUCCA
To Tuscany 1847

Lucca
Pisa

Leghorn

TUSCANY
1860

Siena

Florence

ELBA

CORSICA
To France

SARDINIA

OF

SARDINIA

Cagliari

Ajaccio

Civita Vecchia

ROMAGNA

Bologna

Ravenna

Rimini

SAN MARINO

UMBRIA

PAPAL STATES

THE MARCHES
1860

Ancona

Rome
1870

Tiber

Gaeta

PONTECORVO
To Papal States

BENEVENTO
To Papal States

ABRUZZI

APULIA

Bari

Brindisi

Otranto

CAMPANIA

Naples

Salerno

+ MT. VESUVIUS

KINGDOM

OF THE

TWO

CALABRIA

SICILIES

Reggio

Messina

MT. ETNA +

SICILY

Catania
1860

Syracuse

Palermo

PANTELLERIA

Tyrrhenian Sea

Mediterranean Sea

Adriatic Sea

Ionian Sea

SWITZERLAND

AUSTRIA

TRENTINO

Trent

VENETIA

Vicenza
1866

Venice
1866

Verona

Padua

SAVOY

Lyon

Rhone

Rhone

Drave

Save

Danube

HUNGARY

CARNIOLA

Laibach

Görz
(Gorizia)
Trieste

Fiume

ISTRIA

Pola

CROATIA

DALMATIA

Zara

LISSA

Ragusa

Belgrade

OTTOMAN

EMPIRE

EMPIRE

A-451840-29-1-1-1-A

Copyright by Rand McNally & Company, Made in U.S.A.

GERMANY AND ITALY
Under Napoleon, 1812

North Sea

Elbe River

Rhine River

Danube River

MECKLENBURG

Berlin

Hamburg

Hanover

WESTPHALIA

BERG

NASSAU

WÜRZ.

FRANKFURT

HESSE

ANHALT

SAXONY

Dresden

Prague

Vienna

CONFEDERATION

OF THE

RHINE

BADEN

WÜRT.

BAVARIA

Munich

SWITZERLAND

Trent

Venice

Milano

Turin

ITALY

To France

CORSICA

Rome

NAPLES

Naples

To France

Adriatic Sea

43

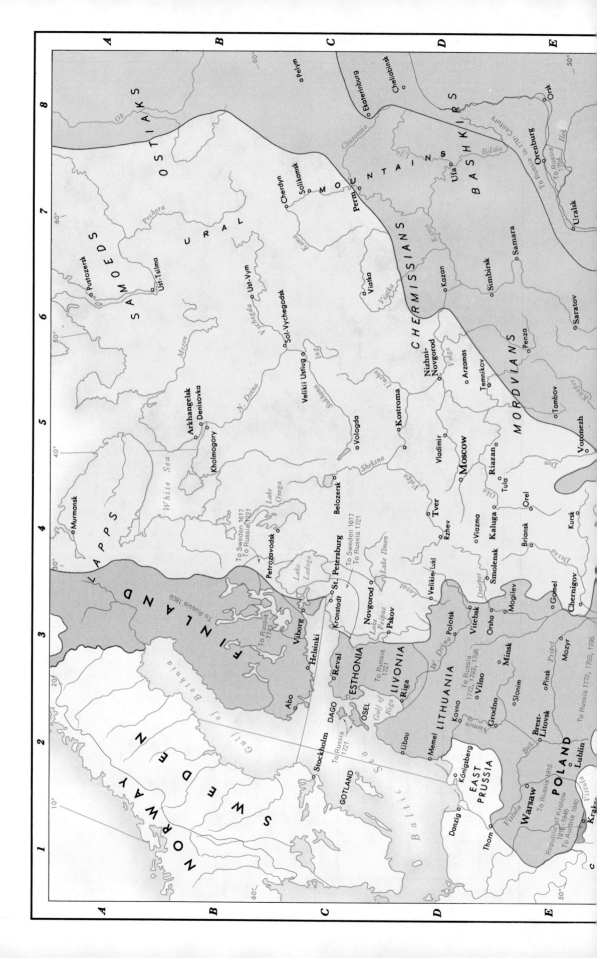

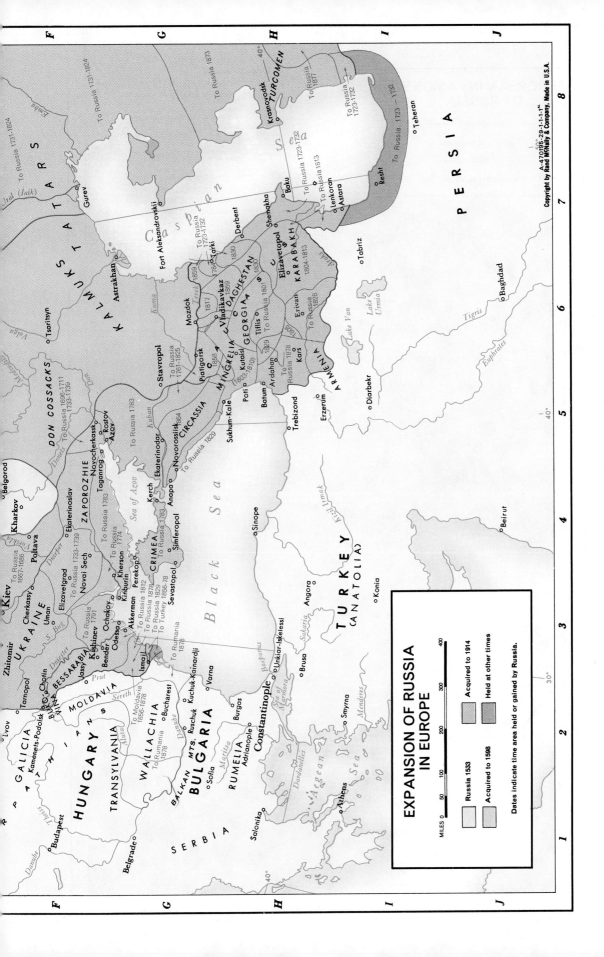

EXPANSION OF RUSSIA
IN EUROPE

MILES 0 50 100 200 300 400

Russia 1533

Acquired to 1598

Acquired to 1914

Held at other times

Dates indicate time area held or gained by Russia.

EUROPEAN INVASIONS OF RUSSIA

MILES 0 50 100 200 300 400

- - - - 1815 Boundaries
———— 1920 Boundaries

States colored as of 1920

INVASIONS OF RUSSIA

INVASION ROUTES

—·—·— Swedish Invasions by Charles XII 1700-1709

———— Napoleon's invasion and retreat from Moscow 1812

- - - - Crimean War—Allied invasion of Evpatorria and battle of Sevastopol

WORLD WAR I

—··—··— British, French, and U.S. intervention in Russia

▭▭▭ Deepest penetrations: (1) German 1918; (2) Polish 1920; and (3) Allied

WORLD WAR II

⋀⋀⋀⋀ German advance to Dec. 1941

⋀⋀⋀⋀ German advance in 1942

∘∘∘∘ Russian front Dec. 1943

●●●● Eastern front Dec. 1944

CRIMEAN WAR

✕ Allied assaults on Russian Coastal areas

A-470196-29-1-1
Copyright by Rand McNally & Company, Made in U.S.A.

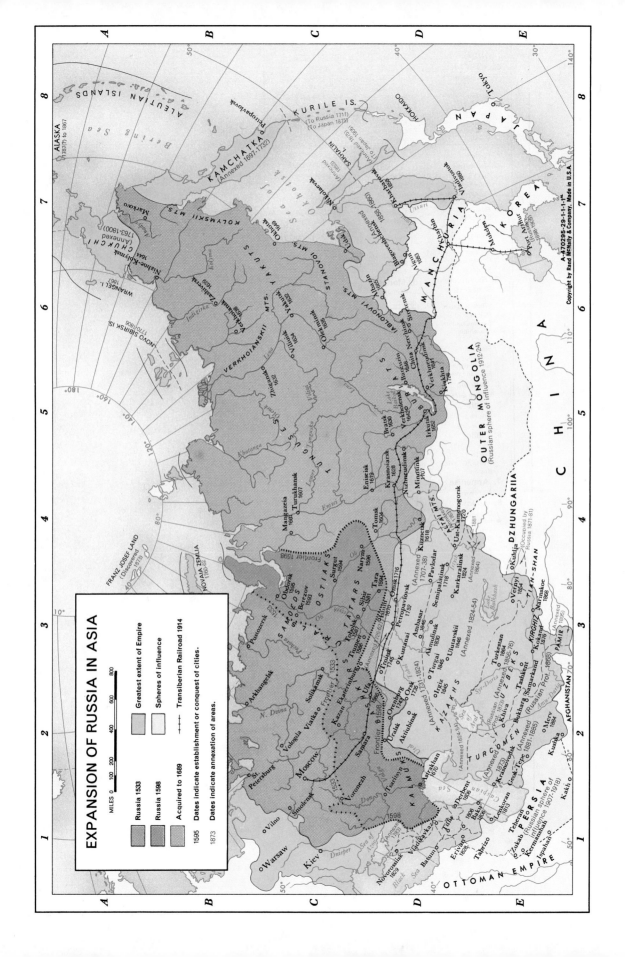

EXPANSION OF RUSSIA IN ASIA

MILES 0 100 200 400 600 800

Russia 1533
Russia 1598
Acquired to 1689

Greatest extent of Empire
Spheres of influence
Transiberian Railroad 1914

1595 ‒†‒ Dates indicate establishment or conquest of cities.

1873 Dates indicate annexation of areas.

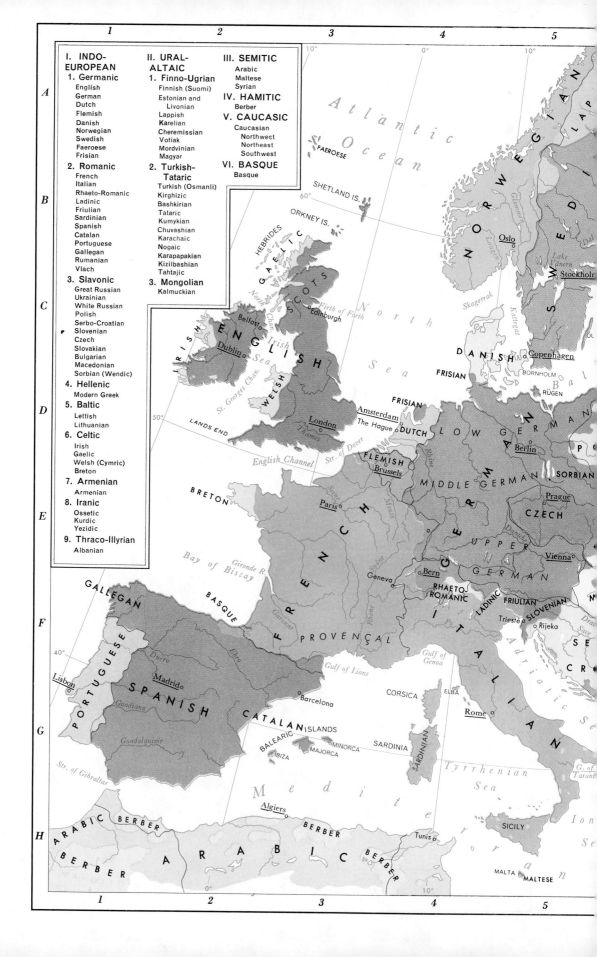

I. INDO-EUROPEAN
 1. Germanic
    English
    German
    Dutch
    Flemish
    Danish
    Norwegian
    Swedish
    Faeroese
    Frisian
 2. Romanic
    French
    Italian
    Rhaeto-Romanic
    Ladinic
    Friulian
    Sardinian
    Spanish
    Catalan
    Portuguese
    Gallegan
    Rumanian
    Vlach
 3. Slavonic
    Great Russian
    Ukrainian
    White Russian
    Polish
    Serbo-Croatian
    Slovenian
    Czech
    Slovakian
    Bulgarian
    Macedonian
    Sorbian (Wendic)
 4. Hellenic
    Modern Greek
 5. Baltic
    Lettish
    Lithuanian
 6. Celtic
    Irish
    Gaelic
    Welsh (Cymric)
    Breton
 7. Armenian
    Armenian
 8. Iranic
    Ossetic
    Kurdic
    Yezidic
 9. Thraco-Illyrian
    Albanian

II. URAL-ALTAIC
 1. Finno-Ugrian
    Finnish (Suomi)
    Estonian and
      Livonian
    Lappish
    Karelian
    Cheremissian
    Votiak
    Mordvinian
    Magyar
 2. Turkish-Tataric
    Turkish (Osmanli)
    Kirghizic
    Bashkirian
    Tataric
    Kumykian
    Chuvashian
    Karachaic
    Nogaic
    Karapapakian
    Kizilbashian
    Tahtajic
 3. Mongolian
    Kalmuckian

III. SEMITIC
    Arabic
    Maltese
    Syrian
IV. HAMITIC
    Berber
V. CAUCASIC
    Caucasian
    Northwest
    Northeast
    Southwest
VI. BASQUE
    Basque

48

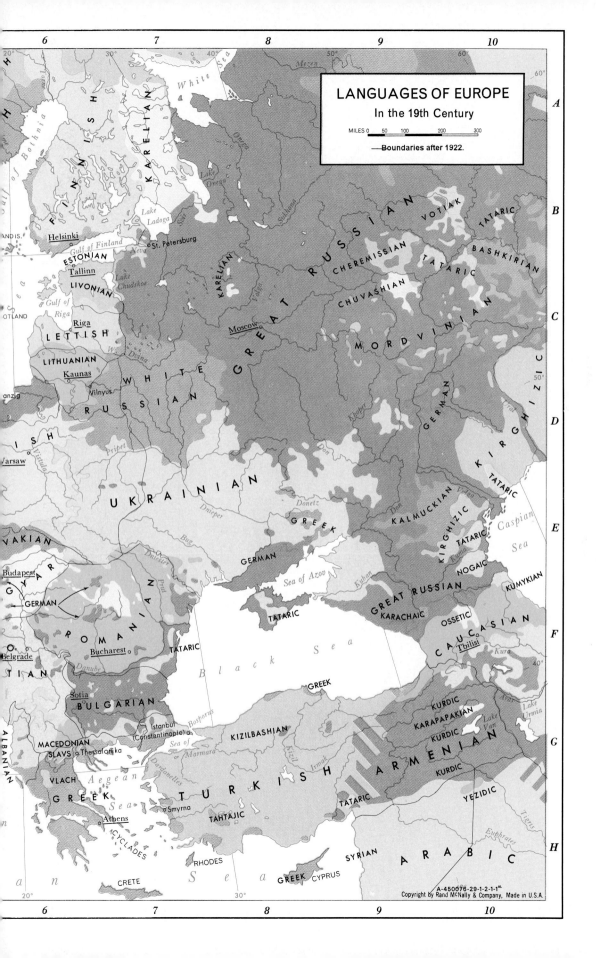

LANGUAGES OF EUROPE
In the 19th Century

MILES 0   50   100   200   300

Boundaries after 1922.

6   7   8   9   10

20°   30°   40°   50°   60°

A

White Sea   *Mezen*   60°

FINNISH   KARELIAN   *Onega*   GREAT RUSSIAN   VOTIAK   TATARIC   B

Lake Ladoga   *Lake Onega*   CHEREMISSIAN   TATARIC   BASHKIRIAN

Helsinki   St. Petersburg   *Neva*   *Sukhona*   CHUVASHIAN   *Volga*

ESTONIAN   *Gulf of Finland*   KARELIAN   GERMAN

Tallinn   *Lake Chudskoe*   *Volga*   MORDVINIAN   C

LIVONIAN   *Gulf of Riga*   Moscow   KIRGHIZIC   50°

LETTISH   Riga   *W. Dvina*   *Kliazma*

LITHUANIAN   WHITE   GERMAN   D

Kaunas   *Pripet*   RUSSIAN   *Don*   TATARIC

Vilnyus   *Volga*

anzig

ISH   UKRAINIAN   *Dnieper*   *Don*   *Volga*   *Ural*   *Caspian Sea*   E

Warsaw   *Bug*   *Donetz*   GREEK   KALMUCKIAN   KIRGHIZIC   TATARIC

Dniester   GERMAN   NOGAIC   KUMYKIAN

VAKIAN   *Sea of Azov*   GREAT RUSSIAN   OSSETIC

GYAR   Budapest   *Prut*   TATARIC   KARACHAIC   CAUCASIAN   F

GERMAN   ROMANIAN   *Kuban*   Tbilisi   40°

O-   Belgrade   Bucharest   TATARIC   *Kura*

TIAN   *Danube*   *Black   Sea*   KURDIC   *Lake Van*   *Aras*   *Lake Irmia*

Sofia   GREEK   KARAPAPAKIAN

BULGARIAN   *Bosporus*   KURDIC   G

MACEDONIAN   Istanbul   KIZILBASHIAN   *Kizil*   *Irmak*   ARMENIAN

ALBANIAN   SLAVS   Thessalonika   (Constantinople)   *Sea of Marmara*   KURDIC

VLACH   *Dardanelles*   TURKISH   YEZIDIC

GREEK   *Aegean Sea*   TATARIC   *Tigris*

Athens   Smyrna   TAHTAJIC   *Euphrates*   H

CYCLADES   SYRIAN   ARABIC

RHODES   *Sea*   GREEK   CYPRUS

CRETE   GREEK

20°   30°

6   7   8   9   10

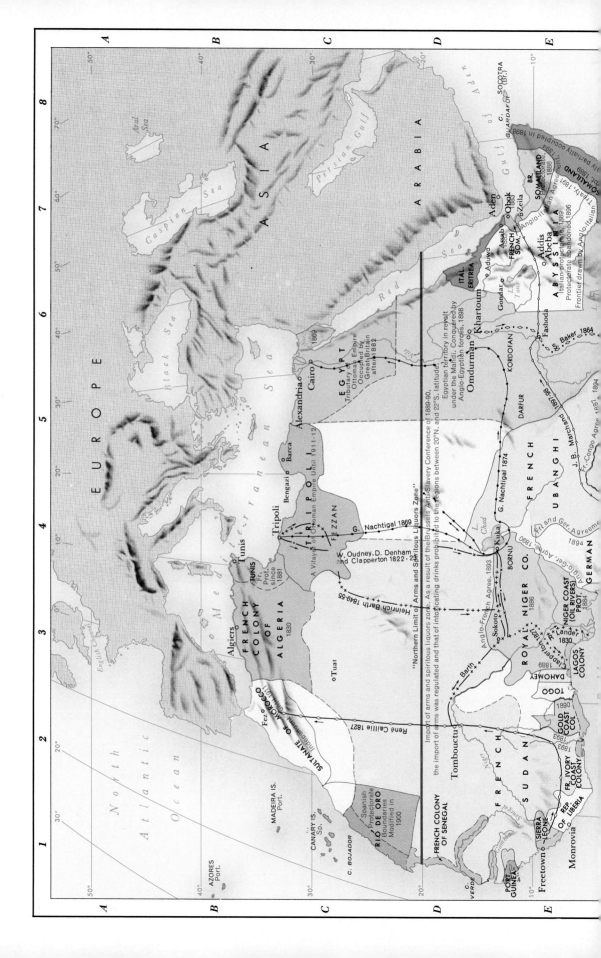

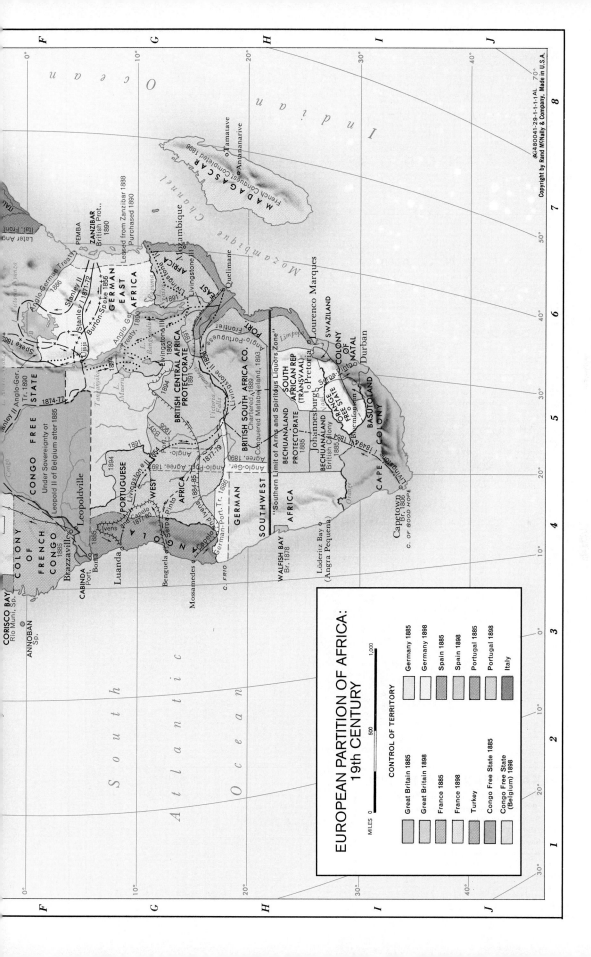

EUROPEAN PARTITION OF AFRICA: 19th CENTURY

CONTROL OF TERRITORY

Great Britain 1885	Germany 1885
Great Britain 1898	Germany 1898
France 1885	Spain 1885
France 1898	Spain 1898
Turkey	Portugal 1885
Congo Free State 1885	Portugal 1898
Congo Free State (Belgium) 1898	Italy

MILES 0   500   1,000

South Atlantic Ocean

Indian Ocean

Mozambique Channel

MADAGASCAR
French Conquest Completed 1896

Antananarive
Tamatave

CORISCO BAY
Rio Muni, Sp.

ANNOBAN
Sp.

COLONY OF FRENCH CONGO 1885

CABINDA Port.

Brazzaville
Leopoldville

CONGO FREE STATE
Under Sovereignty of Leopold II of Belgium after 1885

1874-77

Stanley II Anglo-Ger. Tr. 1890

Anglo-German Treaty 1890

PEMBA

ZANZIBAR
British Prot.
1890
Leased from Zanzibar 1888
Purchased 1890

Stanley II 1886
Stanley I / 1871-72
Burton-Speke 1856
Speke 1862

GERMAN EAST AFRICA

Anglo-Ger. Treaty. 1890

Luanda
PORTUGUESE WEST AFRICA

Benguela Port.
Bonga

Mossamedes

Livingstone II 1854-56
Serpa Pinto 1877-80
Capelo and Ivens 1885
C. FRIO

German-Port. Tr. 1886

Anglo-Port. Agree. 1891

BRITISH CENTRAL AFRICA PROTECTORATE
1891

Mozambique
Livingstone III

Quelimane

Livingstone III 1860

Livingstone II
1894
1895

Victoria Falls

BRITISH SOUTH AFRICA CO.
Chartered, 1889
Conquered Matabeland, 1893

"Southern Limit of Arms and Spirituous Liquors Zone"

Anglo-Ger. Agree., 1890

GERMAN SOUTHWEST AFRICA

WALFISH BAY
Br. 1878

Lüderitz Bay
(Angra Pequena)

Anglo-Port. Frontier

PORT.

Limpopo

Lourenço Marques

SWAZILAND

SOUTH AFRICAN REP.
(TRANSVAAL) 1885

Pretoria
Johannesburg

BECHUANALAND PROTECTORATE
1885

BECHUANALAND British Colony 1885

ORANGE FREE STATE 1854

Bloemfontein

COLONY OF NATAL
Durban

BASUTOLAND

CAPE COLONY

Capetown
Br. 1806
C. OF GOOD HOPE

Livingstone I 1849-51

Italy Front.

Later Ang...

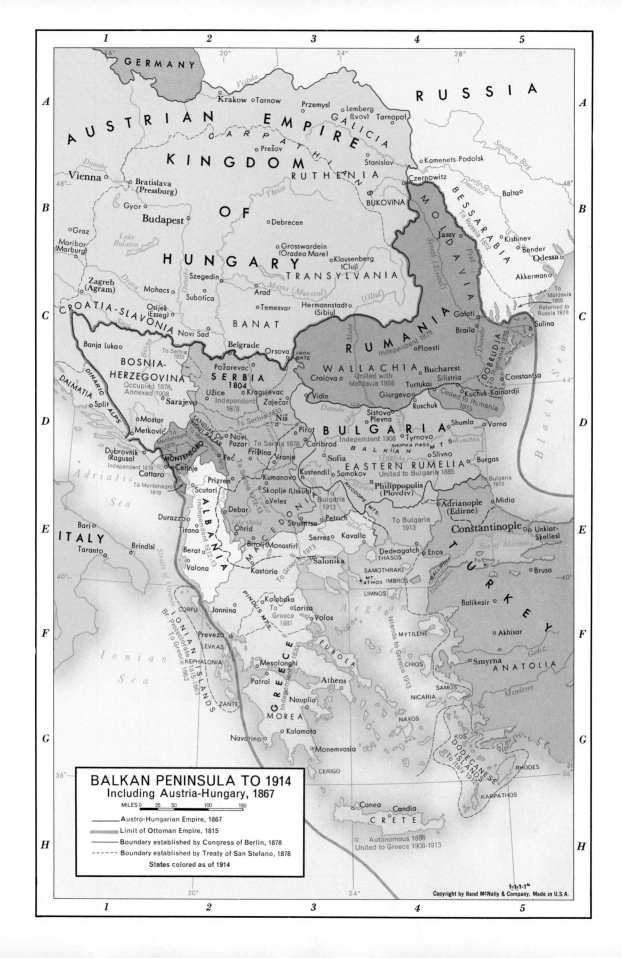

BALKAN PENINSULA TO 1914
Including Austria-Hungary, 1867

MILES 0   25   50   100   150

—————— Austro-Hungarian Empire, 1867

▬▬▬▬▬▬ Limit of Ottoman Empire, 1815

—————— Boundary established by Congress of Berlin, 1878

- - - - - - Boundary established by Treaty of San Stefano, 1878

States colored as of 1914

GERMANY

RUSSIA

AUSTRIAN EMPIRE

KINGDOM

OF

HUNGARY

Vienna
Krakow   Tarnow   Przemysl   Lemberg (Lvov)   Tarnopol
GALICIA
CARPATHIANS
Prešov
Stanislav
RUTHENIA
Czernowitz
Kamenets-Podolsk
Southern Bug
Balta
BUKOVINA
Dniester
BESSARABIA
To Russia 1812
Bratislava (Pressburg)
Gyor
Budapest
Debrecen
Graz
Lake Balaton
Maribor (Marburg)
Grosswardein (Oradea Mare)
Klausenberg (Cluj)
Jassy
MOLDAVIA
Kishinev
Bender
Odessa
Szegedin
TRANSYLVANIA
Akkerman
To Moldavia 1856 Returned to Russia 1878
Zagreb (Agram)
Mohacs
Subotica
Arad
Temesvar
Hermannstadt (Sibiu)
Drava
Maros (Muresul)
Oltul
CROATIA-SLAVONIA
Novi Sad
BANAT
Galati
Sulina
Banja Luka
Belgrade
Orsova
IRON GATE
RUMANIA
Independent 1878
Braila
DOBRUDJA Ceded to Rumania 1878
Black Sea
BOSNIA-HERZEGOVINA
Occupied 1878, Annexed 1908
Požarevac
SERBIA 1804
WALLACHIA
United with Moldavia 1858
Bucharest
DINARIC ALPS
DALMATIA
Sarajevo
Užice
Independent 1878
Kragujevac
Zaječar
To Serbia 1833
Craiova
Vidin
Giurgevo
Turtukai
Silistria
Ruschuk
Constantsa
Split
Mostar
SANDJAK NOVIBAZAR
Nis
To Serbia 1878
Pirot
BULGARIA
Sistova
Plevna
Shumla
Varna
Kuchuk-Kainardji Ceded to Rumania 1913
Metkovic
Montenegro 1878
Novi Pazar
Caribrod
Tyrnovo
Independent 1908
BALKAN MTS.
Danube
Dubrovnik (Ragusa)
Independent 1878
Peć
Priština
Vranje
Sofia
Kustendil
SHIPKA PASS
EASTERN RUMELIA
United to Bulgaria 1885
Slivno
Burgas
To Bulgaria 1913
MONTENEGRO
Cetinje
Cattaro
To Montenegro 1878
Prizren
Kumanovo
Samokov
Philippopolis (Plovdiv)
Adriatic Sea
Scutari
Skoplje (Uskub)
Veles
RHODOPE MTS.
Adrianople (Edirne)
Midia
Durazzo
ALBANIA Independent 1912-13
Debar
Lake Ohrid
To Bulgaria 1913
MACEDONIA
Petrich
Constantinople
Unkiar-Skellesi
Bari
Tirana
Ohrid
Strumitsa
Serres
Kavala
Sea of Marmora
Brusa
Brindisi
Taranto
ITALY
Berat
Bitoli (Monastir)
To Greece 1913
Dedeagatch
Enos
TURKEY
Valona
Kastoria
Salonika
THASOS
SAMOTHRAKI
GALLIPOLI
Balikesir
MT. ATHOS
IMBROS
Dardanelles
Straits of Otranto
Kalabaka To Greece 1881
Larisa
LIMNOS
Akhisar
Br. Protectorate To Greece 1815-1863
CORFU
Jannina
PINDUS MTS.
Volos
Aegean Sea
MYTILENE
Smyrna
ANATOLIA
Gediz
IONIAN ISLANDS
Preveza
LEVKAS
EUBOEA
Islands to Greece 1913
CHIOS
Menderes
KEPHALONIA
GREECE Independent 1830
Mesolonghi
Patrai
Athens
SAMOS
NICARIA
Ionian Sea
ZANTE
Nauplia
MOREA
NAXOS
DODECANESE ISLANDS To Italy 1912
Navarino
Kalamata
Monemvasia
RHODES
CERIGO
KARPATHOS
Canea
Candia
CRETE
Autonomous 1898
United to Greece 1908-1913

Copyright by Rand McNally & Company, Made in U.S.A.

1-1-1-1 AL

52

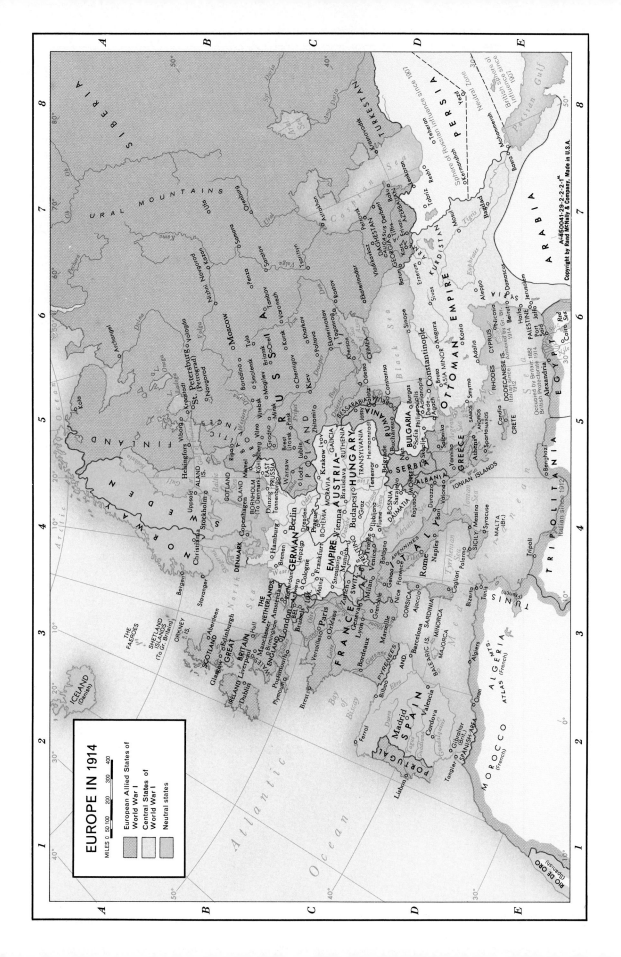

EUROPE IN 1914

MILES 0 50 100 200 300 400

European Allied States of World War I

Central States of World War I

Neutral states

53

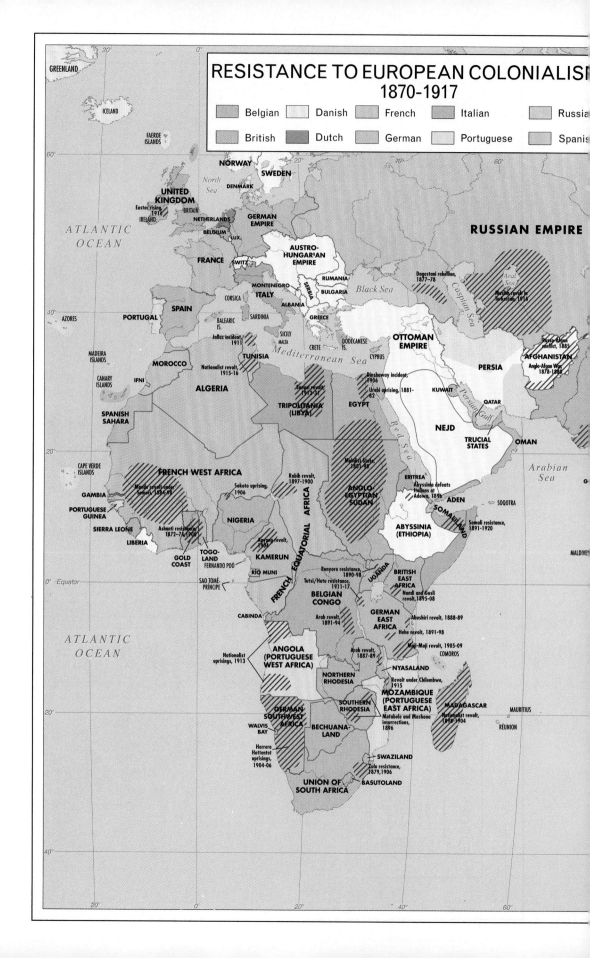

RESISTANCE TO EUROPEAN COLONIALISM
1870-1917

Belgian Danish French Italian Russia[n]

British Dutch German Portuguese Spanis[h]

GREENLAND

ICELAND

FAEROE ISLANDS

ATLANTIC OCEAN

NORWAY

SWEDEN

DENMARK

North Sea

UNITED KINGDOM

Easter rising, 1916
IRELAND BRITAIN

NETHERLANDS
BELGIUM LUX.

GERMAN EMPIRE

AUSTRO-HUNGARIAN EMPIRE

RUSSIAN EMPIRE

FRANCE SWITZ.

MONTENEGRO

SERBIA

RUMANIA

BULGARIA

Black Sea

Aral Sea

Caspian Sea

Dagestani rebellion, 1877-78

Muslim revolt in Turkestan 1916

ITALY

CORSICA

SPAIN

PORTUGAL

AZORES

ALBANIA

SARDINIA

GREECE

SICILY

MALTA

CRETE

DODECANESE IS.

CYPRUS

OTTOMAN EMPIRE

Russo-Afgan conflict, 1885

AFGHANISTAN

Anglo-Afgan War, 1878-1880

PERSIA

BALEARIC IS.

Jallaz incident, 1911

Mediterranean Sea

TUNISIA

Nationalist revolt, 1915-16

MOROCCO

MADEIRA ISLANDS

CANARY ISLANDS

IFNI

ALGERIA

Sanusi revolt, 1912-31

TRIPOLITANIA (LIBYA)

EGYPT

Dinshaway incident, 1906

Urabi uprising, 1881-82

KUWAIT

NEJD

QATAR

TRUCIAL STATES

Persian Gulf

OMAN

Arabian Sea

SPANISH SAHARA

Red Sea

CAPE VERDE ISLANDS

FRENCH WEST AFRICA

Rabih revolt, 1897-1900

Mahdist State, 1881-98

ERITREA

Abyssinia defeats Italians at Adowa, 1896

ADEN

SOQOTRA

GAMBIA

Mande revolt under Samori, 1884-98

Sokoto uprising, 1906

ANGLO-EGYPTIAN SUDAN

SOMALILAND

PORTUGUESE GUINEA

SIERRA LEONE

NIGERIA

Somali resistance, 1891-1920

LIBERIA

Ashanti resistance, 1872-74, 1900

Anyang revolt, 1904

GOLD COAST

TOGO-LAND

FERNANDO POO

KAMERUN

RIO MUNI

FRENCH EQUATORIAL AFRICA

ABYSSINIA (ETHIOPIA)

MALDIVES

SAO TOMÉ-PRINCIPE

Bunyoro resistance, 1890-98

UGANDA

BRITISH EAST AFRICA

Tutsi/Hutu resistance, 1911-17

Nandi and Gusli revolt, 1895-08

CABINDA

BELGIAN CONGO

Arab revolt, 1891-94

GERMAN EAST AFRICA

Abushiri revolt, 1888-89

Hehe revolt, 1891-98

ATLANTIC OCEAN

Arab revolt, 1887-89

Maji-Maji revolt, 1905-09

COMOROS

Nationalist uprisings, 1913

ANGOLA (PORTUGUESE WEST AFRICA)

NYASALAND

Revolt under Chilembwe, 1915

NORTHERN RHODESIA

MOZAMBIQUE (PORTUGUESE EAST AFRICA)

MADAGASCAR

Nationalist revolt, 1895-1904

MAURITIUS

GERMAN SOUTHWEST AFRICA

SOUTHERN RHODESIA

Matabele and Mashona insurrections, 1896

RÉUNION

WALVIS BAY

BECHUANA-LAND

Herrero Hottentot uprisings, 1904-06

SWAZILAND

Zulu resistance, 1879,1906

UNION OF SOUTH AFRICA

BASUTOLAND

Equator

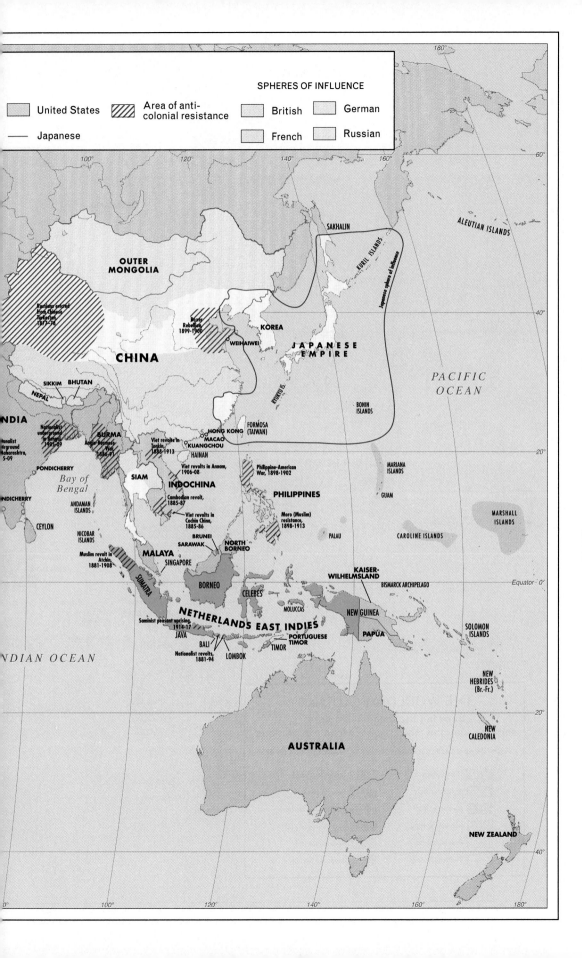

SPHERES OF INFLUENCE

United States

Japanese

Area of anti-colonial resistance

British

French

German

Russian

ALEUTIAN ISLANDS

SAKHALIN

KURIL ISLANDS

Japanese sphere of influence

OUTER MONGOLIA

Russians evicted from Chinese Turkestan 1877-74

Boxer Rebellion 1899-1900

KOREA

CHINA

WEIHAIWEI

JAPANESE EMPIRE

PACIFIC OCEAN

SIKKIM BHUTAN

NEPAL

RYUKYU IS.

BONIN ISLANDS

INDIA

Nationalist underground in Bengal, 1905-09

BURMA

Anglo-Burmese Wars 1885-91

FORMOSA (TAIWAN)

HONG KONG

MACAO

KUANGCHOU

Nationalist underground Maharashtra, 5-09

PONDICHERRY

Viet revolts in Tonkin, 1888-1913

HAINAN

MARIANA ISLANDS

Bay of Bengal

SIAM

INDOCHINA

Viet revolts in Annam, 1906-08

PHILIPPINES

Philippine-American War, 1898-1902

GUAM

PONDICHERRY

ANDAMAN ISLANDS

Cambodian revolt, 1885-87

MARSHALL ISLANDS

CEYLON

NICOBAR ISLANDS

Viet revolts in Cochin China, 1885-86

Moro (Muslim) resistance, 1898-1913

PALAU

CAROLINE ISLANDS

BRUNEI

SARAWAK

NORTH BORNEO

Muslim revolt in Atchin, 1881-1908

MALAYA

SINGAPORE

KAISER-WILHELMSLAND

SUMATRA

BORNEO

CELEBES

BISMARCK ARCHIPELAGO

Equator 0°

MOLUCCAS

NEW GUINEA

Saminist peasant uprising, 1914-17

NETHERLANDS EAST INDIES

SOLOMON ISLANDS

INDIAN OCEAN

JAVA

BALI

TIMOR

PORTUGUESE TIMOR

PAPUA

Nationalist revolts, 1881-94

LOMBOK

NEW HEBRIDES (Br.-Fr.)

NEW CALEDONIA

AUSTRALIA

NEW ZEALAND

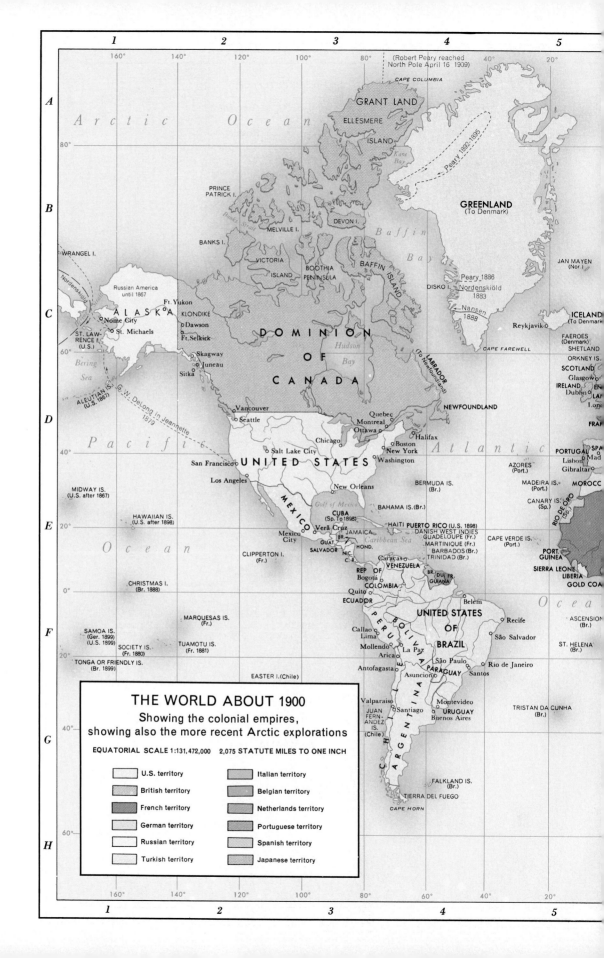

THE WORLD ABOUT 1900

Showing the colonial empires,
showing also the more recent Arctic explorations

EQUATORIAL SCALE 1:131,472,000   2,075 STATUTE MILES TO ONE INCH

U.S. territory		Italian territory	
British territory		Belgian territory	
French territory		Netherlands territory	
German territory		Portuguese territory	
Russian territory		Spanish territory	
Turkish territory		Japanese territory	

Grid references (top): 6   7   8   9   10

20°   40°   60°   80°   100°   120°   140°   160°

A

Arctic Ocean

← Fridtjof Nansen in Fram 1893-1896

80°

FRANZ JOSEF LAND OR
FRIDTJOF NANSEN LAND
(Russia 1928)

NORTHERN LAND
(NICHOLAS II)

NEW SIBERIAN
ISLANDS

DE LONG IS.

B

SPITSBERGEN
(Norway 1920)

Baron   Adolf   Erik

DeLong 1879-1881

WRANGEL
I. (Russia)

BEAR I.
(Nor.)

Barents Sea

1893 - 1896

Nordenskiöld in

Kara Sea

TAIMYR PENINSULA

Nansen

Vega

De Long Strait

1879-1879

NOVAYA ZEMLYA

Nordenskiöld in 1878-1879

Duke of Abruzzi in Stella Polare

Abruzzi 1900

1900

Hammerfest

NORTH CAPE

Vardö

C

KDM. OF
SWEDEN
AND
NORWAY

GR. DUCHY OF
FINLAND

Archangel

RUSSIAN   EMPIRE

60°

Russian Tsar Grand
Duke since 1809

Yakutsk

NORWAY

Christiania

St. Petersburg

Lena

Lofoten

SWEDEN

Goteborg   Stockholm

Tobolsk

Tomsk

Krasnoyarsk

*Sea of
Okhotsk*

D

DEN.

Moscow   Ufa

Kurgan   Omsk

Trans-Siberian   Railway

Irkutsk

Chita

Blagovyeshchensk

SAKHALIN
(Russia 1875)

Petropavlovsk

Hamburg

Samara

Irtysh

Lake Baikal

MONGOLIA

MANCHURIA

Khabarovsk

GER. Berlin   Warsaw

Volga

Aral Sea

Lake Balkhash

Urga

Harbin

Vladivostok

KURILE IS.

EMP.

Vienna
Budapest

AUS.
HUNG.

Odessa

Don

Black Sea

KULJA
(Russia 1871-188-)

EMPIRE

Moukden

Port Arthur
(Russia 1898)

Nordenskiöld 1879

40°

WITZ.

ITALY

SERB.

RUM.

BUL.

Constantinople

Caspian Sea

Merv
(1885)

SINKIANG

Kashgar

OF

Peking

Weihaiwei
(Br. 1898)

KOREA

EMPIRE
OF
JAPAN

Tokyo

Pacific

Rome

Naples

GREECE

TURKISH EMPIRE

CHINA

Ching, Manchu

Tsing Tao
(Ger. 1897)

Yokohama

MALTA
(Br.)

CRETE
(Gr. 1898)

CYPRUS
(Br. 1878)

Teheran

Bagdad

AFG.

Kabul

TIBET

Lhasa

Dynasty since 1644

Shanghai

OGASAWARA IS.
(BONIN IS.)
(Jap. 1878)

TUNIS

Alexandria

PERSIA

Delhi

NEPAL

BHUTAN

CHINA PROPER

Yangtze

RYUKYU IS.
(Jap. 1879)

MARCUS I.
(Jap. 1899)

TRIPOLI
(Turk.)

EGYPT

ARABIA

BALUCH.
1876

BRITISH INDIAN EMPIRE
also many semiautonomous
Indian states
INDIA

BURMA

Macao
(Port.)

Hong
Kong
(Br.)

FORMOSA
(Jap. since 1895)

E

OMAN

Muscat

Mandalay

Kwangchawwan
(Fr. 1898)

20°

SUDAN

Mecca

KURIA
MURIA IS.
(Br.)

GOA
(Port.)

Bombay

Rangoon

FR.
INDO-
CHINA

MARIANAS
(Ger. 1899)

WAKE I.
(U.S. 1898)

NIGERIA

ABYSSINIA

ADEN

SOCOTRA
(1886)

Mahé
(Fr.)

Madras

Pondichéry

LACCADIVE IS.
(Br.)

Calcutta

SIAM

Bangkok

PHILIPPINE
IS.
(U.S. 1899)

GUAM
(U.S. 1898)

MARSHALL IS.
(Ger. 1899)

KAMERUN

ERIT.

FR. SOM.

BR. SOM.

IT. SOM.

CEYLON

MALDIVE IS.
(Br.)

NICOBAR IS.
(Br.)

ANDAMAN IS.
(Br.)

STRAITS
SETTLEMENTS

SARAWAK

N.
BORNEO
(1888)

PELEW IS.
(Ger. 1899)

CAROLINES
(Ger. 1899)

Ocean

GILBERT IS.
(Br. 1899)

CONGO FREE
STATE
Ruled by
Leopold II of
Belgium

GER.
E. AFR.

ZANZIBAR
(Br. 1890)

SEYCHELLES
(Br.)

Singapore

SUMATRA

BORNEO

MOLUCCA

NEW GUINEA
(Neth.
1901)

Ger.
(Ger.
1884)
(Br.
1884)

NEW MECKLENBURG

BISMARCK IS.
(Ger. 1884)

NEW
POMERANIA

ELLICE IS.
(Br. 1892)

ABINDA
(Port.)

Loanda

ANGOLA

E. AFR.

COMORO IS.
(Fr.)

CELEBES

TIMOR
(Port.)

JAVA

Indian

COCOS IS.
(Br. 1876)

TIMOR
(Neth.)

SOLOMON IS.
Div. between
Br. and Ger. 1899

SP.
INEA

RHODESIA

Mozambique

MADAGASCAR
(Fr. 1896)

MAURITIUS (Br.)

Darwin

NEW
HEBRIDES

FIJI IS.
(Br. 1874)

F

GER.
S.W.
AFR.

BECHUANA-
LAND

TRANS-
VAAL

NATAL

PORT. E. AFR.

REUNION (Fr.)

NORTHERN
TERRITORY

COMMONWEALTH   OF

WESTERN
AUSTRALIA

AUSTRALIA
(including Tasmania formed in 1901)

QUEENSLAND

SOUTH
AUSTRALIA

NEW
CALEDONIA
(Fr.)

LOYALTY IS.
(Fr. 1864)

ORANGE
FREE STATE

CAPE
COLONY

Lourenço
Marques

Capetown

Perth

Adelaide

NEW
SOUTH
WALES

VICTORIA

Brisbane

Sydney

Ocean

Melbourne

TASMANIA

Wellington

G

NEW
ZEALAND
Organized as a
Dominion in 1907

60°

H

20°   40°   60°   80°   100°   120°   140°

6   7   8   9   10

EUROPE 1922-40

MILES 0   50 100   200   300

	Principal status quo powers
	Principal Revisionist powers
	1914 Boundaries
	1922 Boundaries

Ocean

Pechenga
MURMAN COAST
Murmansk
KOLA PENINSULA
Archangel

White Sea

Lake Onega
Lake Ladoga

Kronstadt
Leningrad (Petrograd)
Novgorod
Pskov
Vitebsk
Smolensk
Borisov
Minsk
Mogilev
Briansk
Chernigov
Kiev
Zhitomir
Kirovograd (Elizavetgrad)
Odessa
Kishinev
BESSARABIA
ernowitz
UKRAINE

Vologda
Yaroslavl
Kalinin (Tver)
Moscow
Tula Riazan
Orel
Kursk
Kharkov
Poltava
Dnepropetrovsk (Ekaterinoslav)
Taganrog
Rostov

Kirov
Molotov
Gorkii (Nizhni Novgorod)
Kazañ
Penza
Tambov
Saratov
Voronezh
Stalingrad

Sverdlovsk
Cheliabinsk
Magnitogorsk
Ufa
Chkalov   Orsk
Uralsk

Kustanai
Akmolinsk

U R A L   M O U N T A I N S

U N I O N   O F   S O V I E T   S O C I A L I S T   R E P U B L I C S

Pechora
Vychegda
Dvina
Kama
Volga
Belaia
Oka
Don
Dnieper
Bug
Dniester
Pruth

Irtish
Ishim
Tobol
Ural

A S I A
Aral Sea

Astrakhan
Voroshilovsk (Stavropol)
Krasnodar (Ekaterinodar)
Novorossiisk (Anapa)
Sevastopol
Cherson

Sea of Azov
Kubañ
Terek

Grozni
Petrovsk
Ordzhonikidze (Vladikavkaz)
DAGHESTAN
Derbent
Sukhumi
REPUBLIC OF GEORGIA
Poti
Batum
Tiflis
REPUBLIC OF ARMENIA
Erivan
REPUBLIC OF AZERBAIJAN
Baku
Krasnovodsk
Lenkoran

Caspian Sea

T U R K E S T A N

P E R S I A

Sinope
Samsun
Trebizond
Kars
Ankara (Angora)
Tokat
Kizil Irmak
Bry. of Armenia as arbitrated by President Wilson
KURDISTAN

L. Urmia
L. Tabriz

Tabriz
Teheran

T U R K E Y
A S I A   M I N O R

Smyrna
Aidin
Konia
Adana
Line of the treaty of Sèvres
Brdy. between Syria and Turkey as Estab'd by Agree. Aug. 1921
Aleppo
Mosul
ALEXANDRETTA Annexed by Turkey 1939
Latakia
Homs
Brdy. line between Fr. and Br. Mandate as Estab'd by Agree. Dec. 23, 1920
Nikosia
CYPRUS (Br.)
Limasol
S Y R I A
Beirut
Damascus
Ter's. as Estab'd by Agree. Dec. 23, 1920
I R A Q
Independent since 1932
Bagdad

Tigris
Euphrates

Acre
PALESTINE Br. Mandate
Jaffa
Jerusalem
TRANSJORDAN Br. Mandate
Amman
KUWAIT
Kuwait

Persian Gulf

ependent Kingdom with itish Protective Rights
Alexandria
Port Said
Dead Sea
Cairo
Nile
Red Sea
E G Y P T
A R A B I A

Istanbul (Constantinople)
Gallipoli
Brusa
Eregli
Skutari
Makri
RHODES
Adalia

Black Sea
Bosphorus

Varna
Burgas
Constantsa
To Bulgaria 1940
OBRUJA
Galatz
Annexed by USSR 1940

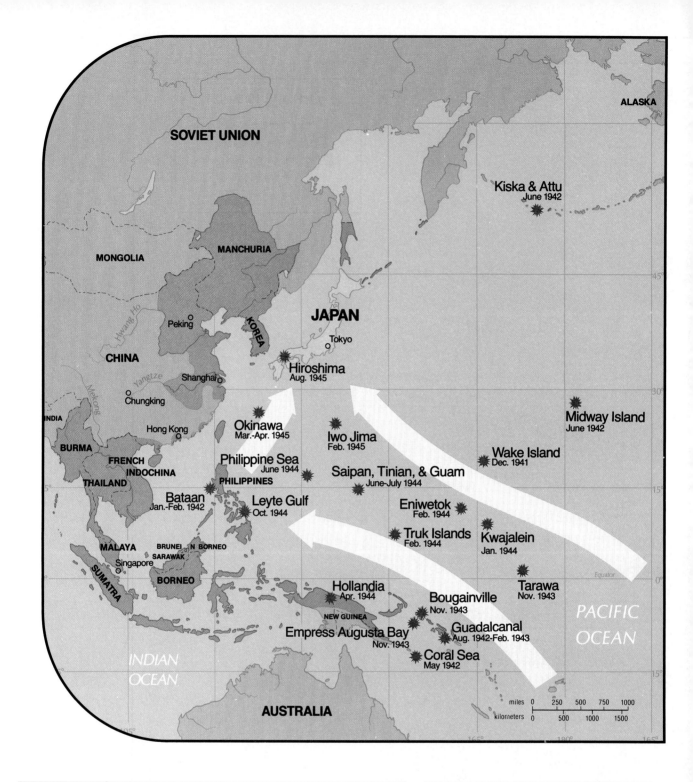

U. S. CASUALTIES IN SECOND WORLD WAR
1941-1946

Branch	Numbers engaged	Battle deaths	Other deaths	Total deaths	Wounds not mortal	Total casualties
Army*	11,260,000	234,874	83,400	318,274	565,861	884,135
Navy	4,183,466	36,950	25,664	62,614	37,778	100,392
Marines	669,100	19,773	4,778	24,511	67,207	91,718
Total	16,112,566	291,557	113,842	405,399	670,846	1,076,245

SECOND WORLD WAR CASUALTIES

Country	Battle Deaths	Wounded
Australia	26,976	180,684
China	1,324,516	1,762,006
India	32,121	64,354
Japan	1,270,000	140,000
New Zealand	11,625	17,000
United Kingdom	357,116	369,267
United States	291,557	670,846

Source: Information Please Almanac (Boston: Houghton Mifflin Co., 1988)

Source: Information Please Almanac (Boston: Houghton Mifflin Co., 1988)

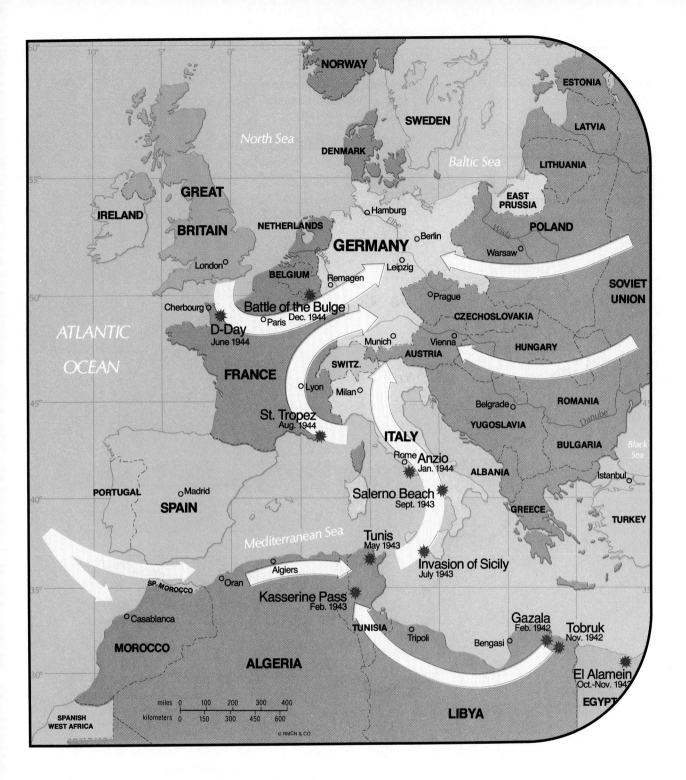

Map labels (European Theatre – WWII):

NORWAY · SWEDEN · ESTONIA · LATVIA · LITHUANIA · DENMARK · East Prussia · POLAND · GREAT BRITAIN · IRELAND · NETHERLANDS · GERMANY · BELGIUM · SOVIET UNION · CZECHOSLOVAKIA · HUNGARY · AUSTRIA · FRANCE · SWITZ. · ROMANIA · YUGOSLAVIA · ITALY · BULGARIA · ALBANIA · GREECE · TURKEY · PORTUGAL · SPAIN · MOROCCO · ALGERIA · TUNISIA · LIBYA · EGYPT · SPANISH WEST AFRICA · SP. MOROCCO

Cities: Hamburg · Berlin · Leipzig · Warsaw · Prague · London · Remagen · Cherbourg · Paris · Munich · Vienna · Lyon · Milan · Belgrade · Rome · Istanbul · Madrid · Oran · Algiers · Casablanca · Tripoli · Bengasi

Seas/Oceans: North Sea · Baltic Sea · ATLANTIC OCEAN · Mediterranean Sea · Black Sea

Rivers: Elbe · Rhine · Wisła · Danube

Battles/Events:
- Battle of the Bulge Dec. 1944
- D-Day June 1944
- St. Tropez Aug. 1944
- Anzio Jan. 1944
- Salerno Beach Sept. 1943
- Tunis May 1943
- Invasion of Sicily July 1943
- Kasserine Pass Feb. 1943
- Gazala Feb. 1942
- Tobruk Nov. 1942
- El Alamein Oct.-Nov. 1942

Scale:
miles 0 100 200 300 400
kilometers 0 150 300 450 600

© RMCN & CO

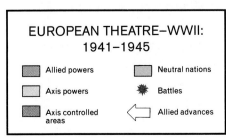

EUROPEAN THEATRE–WWII: 1941–1945

- Allied powers
- Axis powers
- Axis controlled areas
- Neutral nations
- Battles ✸
- Allied advances ⟵

SECOND WORLD WAR CASUALTIES

Country	Battle Deaths	Wounded
Austria	280,000	350,117
Canada	32,714	53,145
France	201,568	400,000
Germany	3,250,000	7,250,000
Hungary	147,435	89,313
Italy	149,496	66,716
Poland	320,000	530,000
U.S.S.R.	6,115,000	14,012,000

Source: Information Please Almanac (Boston: Houghton Mifflin Co., 1988)

1 EAST GERMANY
- **1989** Berlin Wall falls.
- **1990** Germany is reunited.

2 CZECHOSLOVAKIA
- **1989** Coalition government is formed.
- **1990** Free elections are held.
- **1993** Country splits into Czech Republic and Slovakia.

3 POLAND
- **1980** Discontented laborers form Solidarity.
- **1989** Solidarity candidates defeat Communists in elections.

5 HUNGARY
- **1988** Democratic reforms are implemented.
- **1989** Communist party is dissolved.
- **1990** Hungary holds free, multi-party elections.

6 ROMANIA
- **1989** Government is overthrown in a violent uprising.
- **1990** Communist party is banned.

7 BULGARIA
- **1989** Communist leadership resigns.
- **1991** Democratic elections are held.

© Rand McNally & Co.
H-HMW50093-Z1- -1-1-1

62

Breakup of the U.S.S.R.'s Sphere of Influence

Warsaw Pact Countries

Former Union of Soviet Socialist Republics (U.S.S.R.)

Former Czechoslovakia

Other satellite countries

Iron Curtain

Berlin Wall

| 0 | 100 | 200 | 300 | Miles |
| 0 | 200 | | 400 | Kilometers |

U.S.S.R.

1985 Mikhail Gorbachev gains power and institutes glasnost.

1986 Soviet government terminates aid to neighboring communist nations.

1988 War breaks out between Armenia and Azerbaijan.

Nationalist movements emerge in Kazakhstan and the Baltic Republics.

1989 Soviets put down riots in Georgia.

1990 Lithuania unilaterally secedes from the U.S.S.R.

Soviet troops intervene in Armenia/Azerbaijan war.

1991 Russia, Ukraine and Belarus form the Commonwealth of Independent States; U.S.S.R. is dissolved into fifteen independent republics.

RUSSIA

Ob'

Volga

Volga

KAZAKHSTAN

Astana

Lake Balkhash

CASPIAN SEA

ARAL SEA

Baku

AZERBAIJAN

ZER.

UZBEKISTAN

Tashkent

Bishkek

Issyk-Kul

KYRGYZSTAN

CHINA

TAJIKISTAN

Dushanbe

TURKMENISTAN

Ashgabat

Tehrān

IRAN

Kābul

AFGHANISTAN

PAKISTAN

INDIA

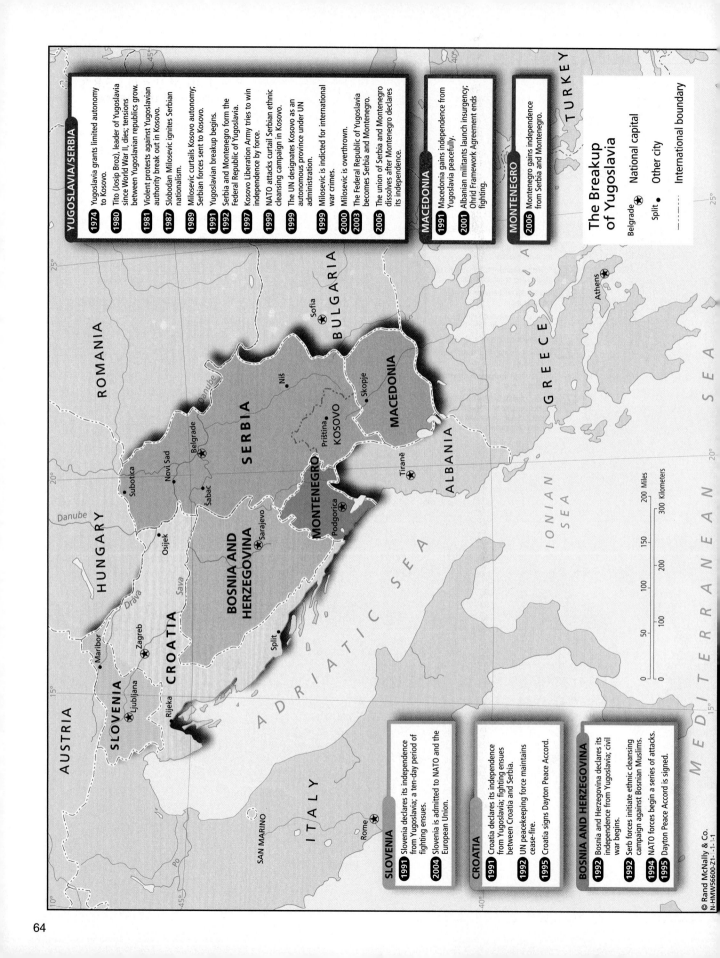

The Breakup of Yugoslavia

YUGOSLAVIA/SERBIA

- **1974** Yugoslavia grants limited autonomy to Kosovo.
- **1980** Tito (Josip Broz), leader of Yugoslavia since World War II, dies; tensions between Yugoslavian republics grow.
- **1981** Violent protests against Yugoslavian authority break out in Kosovo.
- **1987** Slobodan Milosevic ignites Serbian nationalism.
- **1989** Milosevic curtails Kosovo autonomy; Serbian forces sent to Kosovo.
- **1991** Yugoslavian breakup begins.
- **1992** Serbia and Montenegro form the Federal Republic of Yugoslavia.
- **1997** Kosovo Liberation Army tries to win independence by force.
- **1999** NATO attacks curtail Serbian ethnic cleansing campaign in Kosovo.
- **1999** The UN designates Kosovo as an autonomous province under UN administration.
- **1999** Milosevic is indicted for international war crimes.
- **2000** Milosevic is overthrown.
- **2003** The Federal Republic of Yugoslavia becomes Serbia and Montenegro.
- **2006** The union of Serbia and Montenegro dissolves after Montenegro declares its independence.

MACEDONIA

- **1991** Macedonia gains independence from Yugoslavia peacefully.
- **2001** Albanian militants launch insurgency; Ohrid Framework Agreement ends fighting.

MONTENEGRO

- **2006** Montenegro gains independence from Serbia and Montenegro.

SLOVENIA

- **1991** Slovenia declares its independence from Yugoslavia; a ten-day period of fighting ensues.
- **2004** Slovenia is admitted to NATO and the European Union.

CROATIA

- **1991** Croatia declares its independence from Yugoslavia; fighting ensues between Croatia and Serbia.
- **1992** UN peacekeeping force maintains cease-fire.
- **1995** Croatia signs Dayton Peace Accord.

BOSNIA AND HERZEGOVINA

- **1992** Bosnia and Herzegovina declares its independence from Yugoslavia; civil war begins.
- **1992** Serb forces initiate ethnic cleansing campaign against Bosnian Muslims.
- **1994** NATO forces begin a series of attacks.
- **1995** Dayton Peace Accord is signed.

Belgrade ⊛ National capital

Split ● Other city

- - - - - International boundary

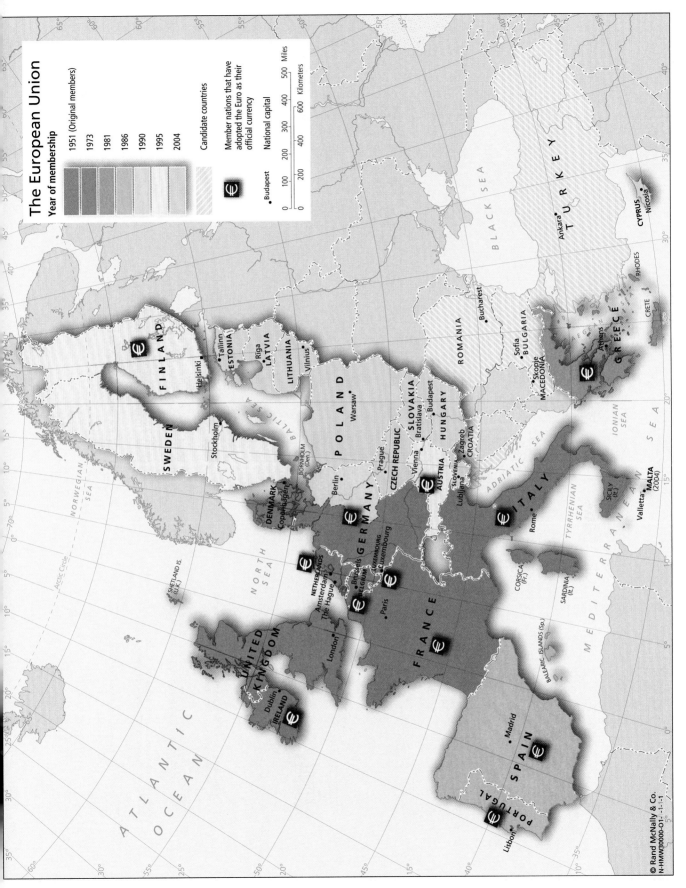

The European Union

Year of membership

1951 (Original members)
1973
1981
1986
1990
1995
2004

Candidate countries

Member nations that have adopted the Euro as their official currency

● Budapest   National capital

Miles
0   100   200   300   400   500
Kilometers
0   200   400   600

© Rand McNally & Co.
N-HMW30000-O1: -1-:-1

ATLANTIC OCEAN

NORWEGIAN SEA

NORTH SEA

BALTIC SEA

Arctic Circle

SHETLAND IS. (U.K.)

UNITED KINGDOM
● London
IRELAND
● Dublin

FINLAND
● Helsinki
SWEDEN
● Stockholm

DENMARK
● Copenhagen
BORNHOLM (Den.)

ESTONIA
● Tallinn
LATVIA
● Riga
LITHUANIA
● Vilnius

NETHERLANDS
Amsterdam
The Hague ●
BELGIUM
● Brussels
LUXEMBOURG
● Luxembourg

GERMANY
● Berlin

POLAND
● Warsaw

CZECH REPUBLIC
● Prague

FRANCE
● Paris

SLOVAKIA
● Bratislava
AUSTRIA
● Vienna
HUNGARY
● Budapest

SLOVENIA
● Ljubljana
CROATIA
● Zagreb

ROMANIA
● Bucharest

BLACK SEA

SPAIN
● Madrid
PORTUGAL
● Lisbon

BALEARIC ISLANDS (Sp.)

CORSICA (Fr.)

SARDINIA (It.)

ITALY
● Rome

TYRRHENIAN SEA

SICILY (It.)

MALTA (2004)
● Valletta

ADRIATIC SEA

BULGARIA
● Sofia
MACEDONIA
● Skopje

GREECE
● Athens

AEGEAN SEA

IONIAN SEA

MEDITERRANEAN SEA

TURKEY
● Ankara

CYPRUS
● Nicosia

RHODES

CRETE

ATLANTIC OCEAN

65

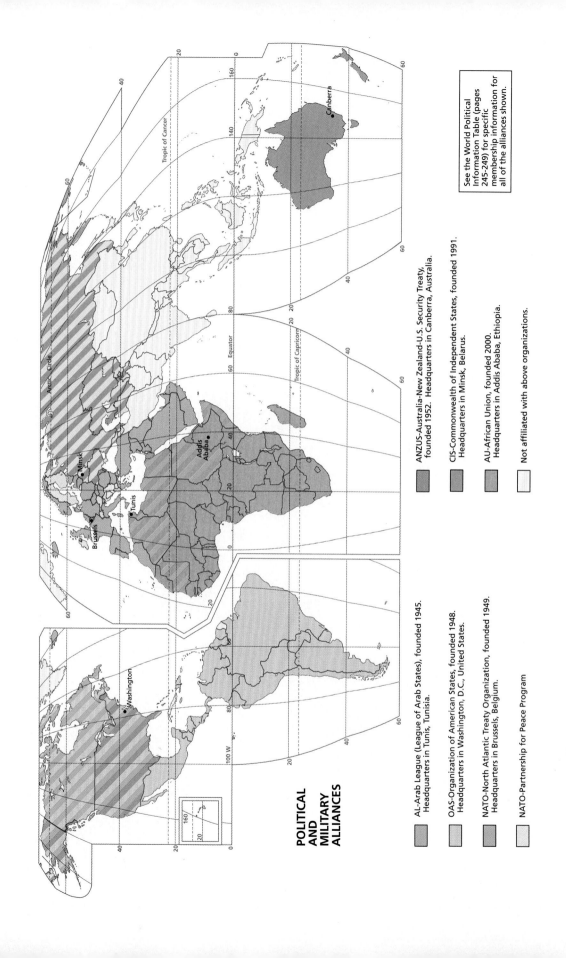

POLITICAL AND MILITARY ALLIANCES

AL–Arab League (League of Arab States), founded 1945. Headquarters in Tunis, Tunisia.

OAS–Organization of American States, founded 1948. Headquarters in Washington, D.C., United States.

NATO–North Atlantic Treaty Organization, founded 1949. Headquarters in Brussels, Belgium.

NATO–Partnership for Peace Program

ANZUS–Australia–New Zealand–U.S. Security Treaty, founded 1952. Headquarters in Canberra, Australia.

CIS–Commonwealth of Independent States, founded 1991. Headquarters in Minsk, Belarus.

AU–African Union, founded 2000. Headquarters in Addis Ababa, Ethiopia.

Not affiliated with above organizations.

See the World Political Information Table (pages 245–249) for specific membership information for all of the alliances shown.

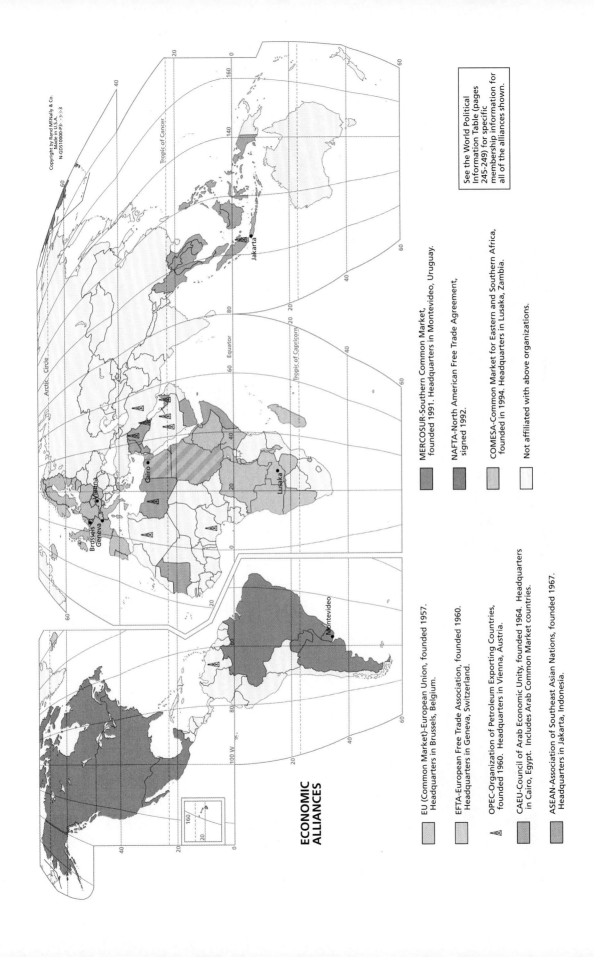

ECONOMIC ALLIANCES

EU (Common Market)-European Union, founded 1957. Headquarters in Brussels, Belgium.

EFTA-European Free Trade Association, founded 1960. Headquarters in Geneva, Switzerland.

OPEC-Organization of Petroleum Exporting Countries, founded 1960. Headquarters in Vienna, Austria.

CAEU-Council of Arab Economic Unity, founded 1964. Headquarters in Cairo, Egypt. Includes Arab Common Market countries.

ASEAN-Association of Southeast Asian Nations, founded 1967. Headquarters in Jakarta, Indonesia.

MERCOSUR-Southern Common Market, founded 1991. Headquarters in Montevideo, Uruguay.

NAFTA-North American Free Trade Agreement, signed 1992.

COMESA-Common Market for Eastern and Southern Africa, founded in 1994. Headquarters in Lusaka, Zambia.

Not affiliated with above organizations.

See the World Political Information Table (pages 245-249) for specific membership information for all of the alliances shown.

Copyright by Rand McNally & Co.
Made in U.S.A.
N-GDS10000-P3-·>·3-3

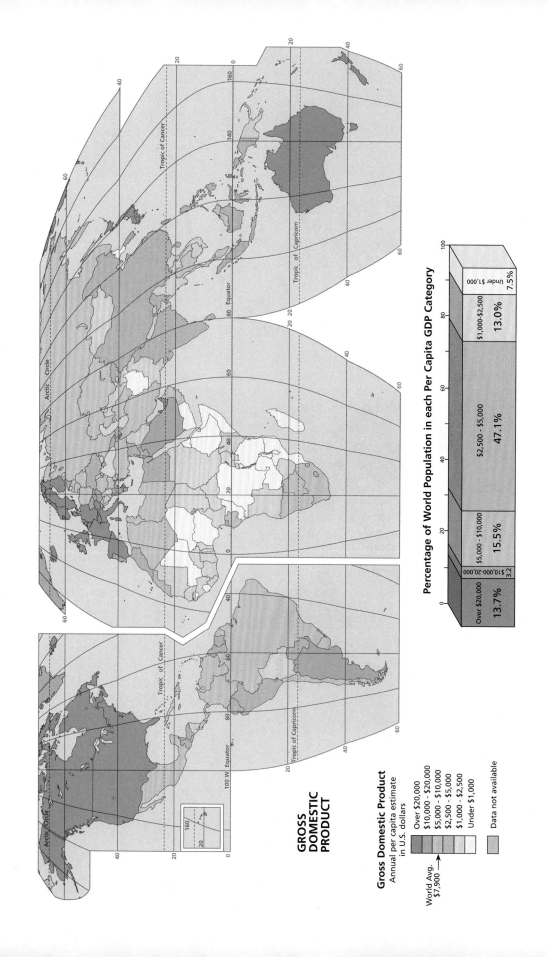

GROSS DOMESTIC PRODUCT

Gross Domestic Product
Annual per capita estimate
in U.S. dollars

Over $20,000
$10,000 - $20,000
$5,000 - $10,000
$2,500 - $5,000
$1,000 - $2,500
Under $1,000

World Avg. → $7,900

Data not available

Percentage of World Population in each Per Capita GDP Category

Over $20,000 — 13.7%
$10,000-20,000 — 3.2
$5,000 - $10,000 — 15.5%
$2,500 - $5,000 — 47.1%
$1,000-$2,500 — 13.0%
Under $1,000 — 7.5%

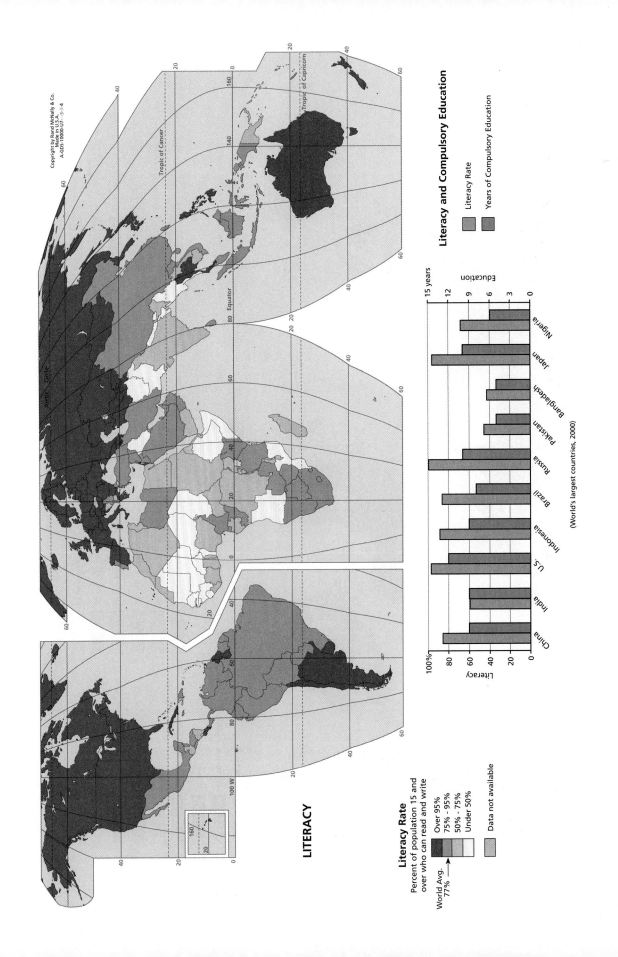

LITERACY

Literacy Rate

Percent of population 15 and over who can read and write

- Over 95%
- 75% – 95%
- 50% – 75%
- Under 50%
- Data not available

World Avg. 77%

Literacy and Compulsory Education

- Literacy Rate
- Years of Compulsory Education

(World's largest countries, 2000)

Copyright by Rand McNally & Co.
Made in U.S.A.
A-GDS-10000-U7-3-3-4

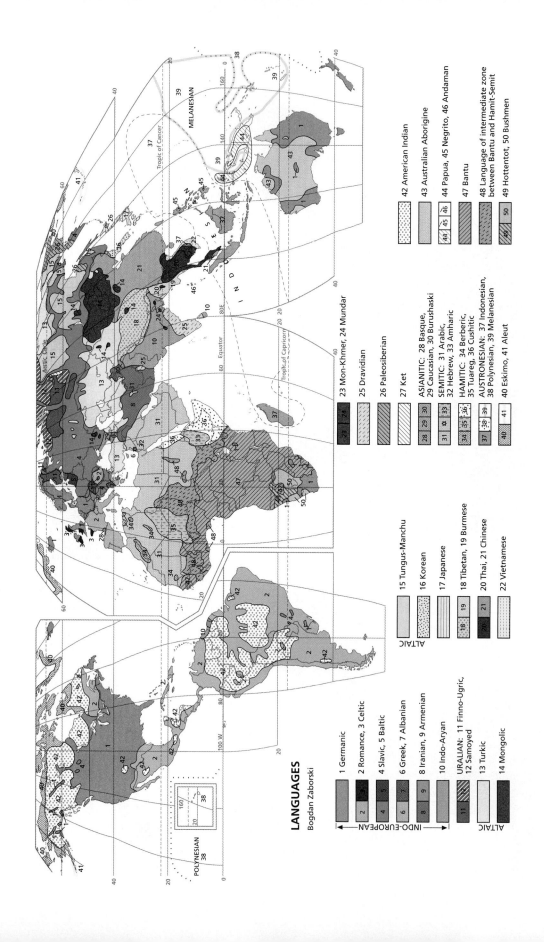

LANGUAGES
Bogdan Zaborski

INDO-EUROPEAN
1 Germanic
2 Romance, 3 Celtic
4 Slavic, 5 Baltic
6 Greek, 7 Albanian
8 Iranian, 9 Armenian
10 Indo-Aryan

URALIAN: 11 Finno-Ugric,
12 Samoyed

ALTAIC
13 Turkic
14 Mongolic

ALTAIC
15 Tungus-Manchu
16 Korean
17 Japanese
18 Tibetan, 19 Burmese
20 Thai, 21 Chinese
22 Vietnamese

23 Mon-Khmer, 24 Mundar
25 Dravidian
26 Paleosiberian
27 Ket

ASIANITIC: 28 Basque,
29 Caucasian, 30 Burushaski
SEMITIC: 31 Arabic,
32 Hebrew, 33 Amharic
HAMITIC: 34 Berberic,
35 Tuareg, 36 Cushitic
AUSTRONESIAN: 37 Indonesian,
38 Polynesian, 39 Melanesian
40 Eskimo, 41 Aleut

42 American Indian
43 Australian Aborigine
44 Papua, 45 Negrito, 46 Andaman
47 Bantu
48 Language of intermediate zone
between Bantu and Hamit-Semit
49 Hottentot, 50 Bushmen

POLYNESIAN
38

MELANESIAN

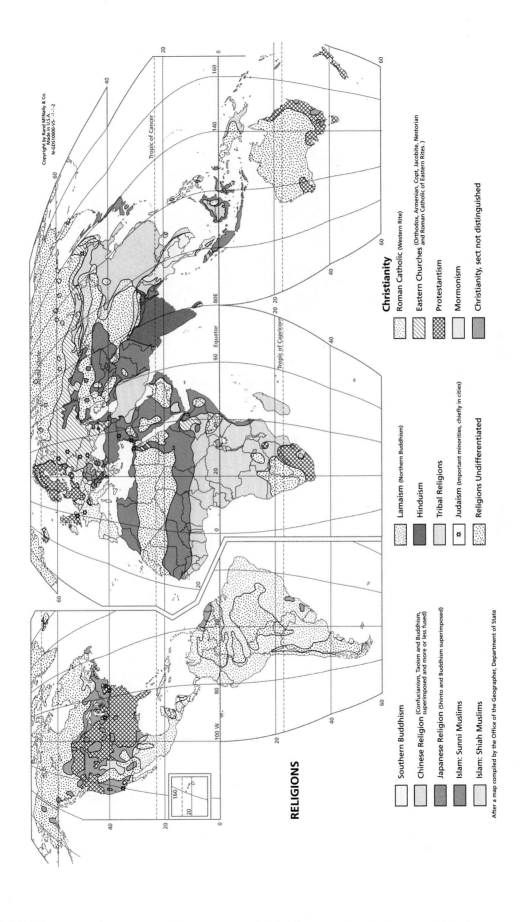

RELIGIONS

Southern Buddhism

Chinese Religion (Confucianism, Taoism and Buddhism, superimposed and more or less fused)

Japanese Religion (Shinto and Buddhism superimposed)

Islam: Sunni Muslims

Islam: Shiah Muslims

Lamaism (Northern Buddhism)

Hinduism

Tribal Religions

Judaism (Important minorities, chiefly in cities)

Religions Undifferentiated

Christianity

Roman Catholic (Western Rite)

Eastern Churches (Orthodox, Armenian, Copt, Jacobite, Nestorian and Roman Catholic of Eastern Rites.)

Protestantism

Mormonism

Christianity, sect not distinguished

After a map compiled by the Office of the Geographer, Department of State

Copyright by Rand McNally & Co.
Made in U.S.A.
N-GD510000-VS--1--1--2

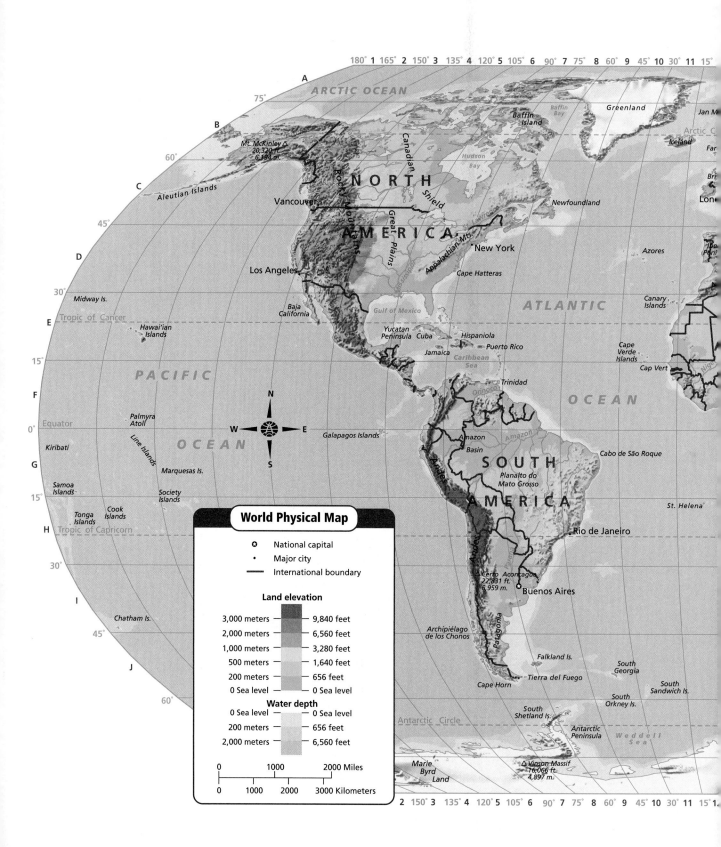

World Physical Map

○ National capital
• Major city
— International boundary

Land elevation

3,000 meters	9,840 feet
2,000 meters	6,560 feet
1,000 meters	3,280 feet
500 meters	1,640 feet
200 meters	656 feet
0 Sea level	0 Sea level

Water depth

0 Sea level	0 Sea level
200 meters	656 feet
2,000 meters	6,560 feet

0   1000   2000 Miles
0   1000   2000   3000 Kilometers

ARCTIC OCEAN

Greenland

Baffin Bay

Baffin Island

Jan M

Iceland

Arctic C

Far

Mt. McKinley △
20,320 ft.
6,194 m.

Canadian Shield

Hudson Bay

Bri

Lon

NORTH AMERICA

Aleutian Islands

Rocky Mountains

Great Plains

Newfoundland

Vancouver

Appalachian Mts.

New York

Cape Hatteras

Azores

The Peni

ATLANTIC

Los Angeles

Midway Is.

Baja California

Tropic of Cancer

Gulf of Mexico

Canary Islands

Hawai'ian Islands

Yucatan Peninsula

Cuba

Hispaniola

Puerto Rico

Jamaica

Caribbean Sea

Cape Verde Islands

Cap Vert

Nig

PACIFIC

Trinidad

Orinoco

OCEAN

Palmyra Atoll

Line Islands

Equator

Galapagos Islands

Amazon Basin

Amazon

Cabo de São Roque

Kiribati

SOUTH

Marquesas Is.

Planalto do Mato Grosso

St. Helena

Samoa Islands

Society Islands

AMERICA

Tonga Islands

Cook Islands

Tropic of Capricorn

Rio de Janeiro

Cerro Aconcagua
22,831 ft.
6,959 m.

Buenos Aires

Chatham Is.

Andes

Archipiélago de los Chonos

Patagonia

Falkland Is.

South Georgia

South Sandwich Is.

Cape Horn

Tierra del Fuego

South Orkney Is.

South Shetland Is.

Antarctic Circle

Antarctic Peninsula

Weddell Sea

Marie Byrd Land

Vinson Massif
16,066 ft.
4,897 m.

ARCTIC OCEAN

A

75°

Franz
Josef Land

sbergen

Nordkapp

Novaya
Zemlya

B

S i b e r i a

60°

Yenisey

Bering

Sea

Scandinavia

Ob

Ural Mts.

Sea of Okhotsk

Kamchatka
Peninsula

C

E

P

Volga

Moscow

Sakhalin

45°

Don

Aral

R

Hokkaidō

D

Caucasus

Black Sea

Gora Elbrus
18,510 ft.
5,642 m.

Beijing

Gobi Desert

Honshū

Sea of Japan

Sardinia

30°

Sicily

Crete

Cyprus

Plateau
of
Tibet

Himalayas

Zagros Mts.

East
China
Sea

Kyūshū

Cairo

Mt. Everest
29,028 ft.
8,848 m.

PACIFIC

Tropic of Cancer

E

a h a r a

R I C A

Arabian
Peninsula

Mumbai
(Bombay)

Decan

Taiwan

Mariana
Islands

Wake
Island

15°

Sahel

Red Sea

Arabian
Sea

Bay of
Bengal

Hainan Dao

South China
Sea

Luzon

Guam

Socotra

Lakshadweep

OCEAN

F

Ethiopian
Plateau

Sri Lanka

Mindanao

Palau
Islands

Caroline
Islands

Marshall
Islands

f of
nea

Congo

Malay
Peninsula

Maldive
Islands

Equator

0°

Congo
Basin

Kilimanjaro
19,340 ft.
5,895 m.

Seychelles

Sumatra

Borneo

Celebes

Java

New Guinea

Solomon
Islands

G

INDIAN

Cocos
Islands

15°

Madagascar

Coral Sea

New
Hebrides

Mauritius

New Caledonia

Fiji
Is.

Reunion

Kalahari
Desert

OCEAN

Great
Sandy
Desert

AUSTRALIA

Tropic of Capricorn

H

Johannesburg

30°

ape of Good Hope

Darling

Great Dividing Range

Sydney

Cape Leeuwin

Aoraki
(Mt. Cook)
12,316 ft.
3,754 m.

North Island

I

Tasmania

South Island

45°

Îles Kerguélen

J

60°

SOUTHERN

OCEAN

Antarctic Circle

K

ueen Maud
Land

Enderby
Land

Wilkes Land

Victoria Land

75°

L

ANTARCTICA

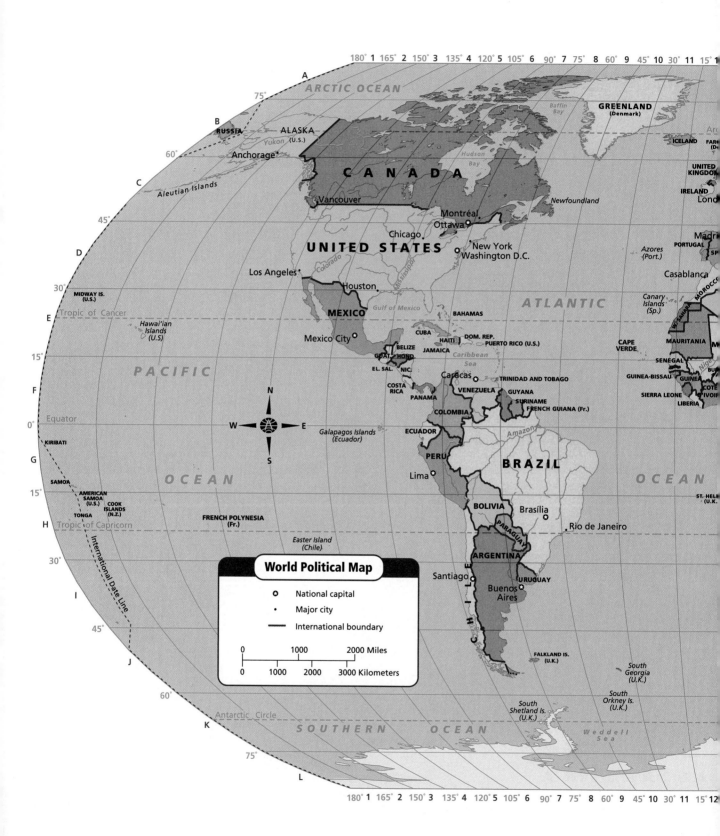

World Political Map

⊙ National capital

• Major city

— International boundary

0	1000	2000 Miles
0	1000	2000	3000 Kilometers

15° 14 30° 15 45° 16 60° 17 75° 18 90° 19 105° 20 120° 21 135° 22 150° 23 165° 24 180°

Franz Josef Land

ARCTIC OCEAN

A

75°

bergen (or.)

Novaya Zemlya

B

Yenisey

Lena

60°

Bering Sea

C

R U S S I A

Volga

Moscow

Novosibirsk

Sea of Okhotsk

NORWAY

FINLAND

SWEDEN **EST.**

DEN. **LAT.**

GERMANY **LITH.**

POLAND **BELARUS**

CZ. **UKRAINE**

AUS. **HUNG.**

ITALY **ROM.**

Rome **SERB.** **BUL.**

ALB.

GREECE **TURKEY**

TUNISIA *Crete* **CYPRUS** **SYRIA**

ISRAEL **LEB.**

JORDAN

GEO. **AZER.**

ARM.

UZBEKISTAN **KYRG.**

TURKMENISTAN **TAJIK.**

KAZAKHSTAN **MONGOLIA**

NORTH KOREA

Beijing **SOUTH KOREA**

Seoul

JAPAN

Tōkyō

45°

C H I N A

Tehrān **AFGHANISTAN**

IRAN

Ob'

Black Sea

Caspian Sea

Mediterranean Sea

IRAQ **KUWAIT**

Cairo

LIBYA **EGYPT** **SAUDI ARABIA** **QATAR**

U.A.E.

Karachi

PAKISTAN

Ganges

NEPAL

BHU.

BNG.

Kolkata (Calcutta)

MYANMAR **LAOS**

Yangtze

Shanghai

TAIWAN

Hong Kong

PACIFIC

D

30°

Tropic of Cancer

E

International Date Line

NIGER **CHAD** **SUDAN**

Addis Ababa **DJIBOUTI**

ERITREA

YEMEN

Red Sea

Nile

OMAN

Mumbai (Bombay)

I N D I A

Arabian Sea

Bay of Bengal

THAILAND

Bangkok

CAMBODIA

VIETNAM

PHILIPPINES

Manila

NORTHERN MARIANA ISLANDS (U.S.)

GUAM (U.S.)

WAKE ISLAND (U.S.)

15°

O C E A N

NIGERIA **CENTRAL AFRICAN REPUBLIC**

Lagos

CAMEROON

EQUATORIAL GUINEA

GABON

Congo

DEM. REP. OF THE CONGO

UGANDA

RWANDA

BURUNDI

KENYA

SOMALIA

ETHIOPIA

SRI LANKA

MALDIVES

SEYCHELLES

BRUNEI

MALAYSIA

SINGAPORE

Borneo

Sumatra

Java

Jakarta

INDONESIA

EAST TIMOR

New Guinea

PAPUA NEW GUINEA

PALAU

FED. STATES OF MICRONESIA

MARSHALL ISLANDS

SOLOMON ISLANDS

Equator

0°

F

G

ANGOLA **ZAMBIA**

TANZANIA

COMOROS

MOZAMBIQUE

MALAWI

ZIMBABWE

NAMIBIA **BOTSWANA**

Johannesburg **SWAZILAND**

SOUTH AFRICA **LESOTHO**

MADAGASCAR

MAURITIUS

REUNION (Fr.)

I N D I A N

O C E A N

Coral Sea

VANUATU

NEW CALEDONIA (Fr.)

FIJI

Tropic of Capricorn

15°

H

A U S T R A L I A

Brisbane

Perth

Darling

Sydney

Auckland

Melbourne

NEW ZEALAND

Tasmania

30°

I

Îles Kerguélen (Fr.)

45°

J

S O U T H E R N **O C E A N**

Antarctic Circle

60°

K

75°

A N T A R C T I C A

© Rand McNally & Co.
Made in U.S.A.
N-CLA10000-P1- -9-9-11

L

15° 14 30° 15 45° 16 60° 17 75° 18 90° 19 105° 20 120° 21 135° 22 150° 23 165° 24 180°

Index

The following index lists important place names appearing on the maps in the *Atlas of Western Civilization*. Countries and regions are indexed to the several maps which portray their areal and political development at successive periods. In general, each index entry includes a map reference key and the page number of the map. Alternate names and spellings are added in parentheses.

ipal Cities of the World

Metropolitan area populations are shown in parentheses.
** City is located within the metropolitan area of another city; for example, Kyōto, Japan is located in the Ōsaka metropolitan area.*

ote d'Ivoire 1,929,079
ana (1,390,000) 949,113
ba, Ethiopia
00) 2,084,588
Australia
54) 16,115
ād, India
78) 3,515,361
ria (Al
larīyah), Egypt
,000) 2,926,859
(El Djazaïr),
ria
7,983) 1,507,241
ty, Kazakhstan
90,000) 1,156,200
mān, Jordan
1,500,000) 963,490
msterdam, Netherlands
(1,121,303) 727,053
nkara (Angora), Turkey
(2,650,000) 2,559,471
ntananarivo,
Madagascar 1,250,000
Antwerp (Antwerpen),
Belgium (1,140,000) 467,518
Asmera, Eritrea 358,100
Asunción, Paraguay
(700,000) 502,426
Athens (Athínai), Greece
(3,150,000) 772,072
Atlanta, Georgia, U.S.
(3,746,400) 416,474
Auckland, New Zealand
(855,571) 315,668
Baghdād, Iraq 3,841,268
Baku (Bakı), Azerbaijan
(2,020,000) 1,080,500
Baltimore, Maryland,
U.S. (2,256,200) 651,154
Bamako, Mali 658,275
Bandung, Indonesia
(2,220,000) 2,058,122
Bangalore, India
(5,686,844) 4,292,223
Bangkok (Krung Thep),
Thailand (7,060,000) 5,620,591
Barcelona, Spain
(4,000,000) 1,496,266
Beijing (Peking), China
(7,320,000) 6,690,000
Beirut, Lebanon
(1,675,000) 509,000
elém, Brazil (965,000) 140,337
elfast, N. Ireland, U.K.
(730,000) 296,700
Belgrade (Beograd),
Serbia and Montenegro
1,554,826) 1,136,786
elo Horizonte, Brazil
(4,055,000) 1,366,301
erlin, Germany
(4,220,000) 3,425,759
irmingham, England, U.K.
(2,705,000) 965,928
ishkek, Kyrgyzstan 631,300
ogotá, Colombia
(5,290,000) 4,931,796
n, Germany
,000) 304,841
n, Massachusetts,
(4,714,000) 589,141
lia, Brazil 1,947,133
islava, Slovakia 451,395
zzaville, Congo 693,712
emen, Germany
790,000) 546,698
risbane, Australia
(1,488,883) 806,746
Brussels (Bruxelles),
Belgium (2,385,000) 136,424
Bucharest (Bucureşti),
Romania (2,300,000) 2,067,545
Budapest, Hungary
(2,450,000) 1,906,798
Buenos Aires, Argentina
(11,000,000) 2,960,976
Cairo (Al Qāhirah), Egypt
(9,300,000) 6,068,695
Cali, Colombia
(1,735,000) 1,641,498
Canberra, Australia
(324,536) 298,847
Cape Town, South Africa
(1,900,000) 854,616
Caracas, Venezuela
(4,000,000) 1,822,465
Casablanca, Morocco
(3,400,000) 3,022,000
Changchun, China 2,470,000
Chelyabinsk, Russia
(1,320,000) 1,086,300
Chengdu, China 2,760,000
Chennai (Madras), India
(6,424,624) 4,216,268
Chicago, Illinois, U.S.
(8,854,900) 2,896,016

Chişinău (Kishinev),
Moldova 676,700
Chittagong, Bangladesh
(2,342,662) 1,566,070
Chongqing (Chungking),
China 3,870,000
Cincinnati, Ohio, U.S.
(1,704,900) 331,285
Cleveland, Ohio, U.S.
(2,186,200) 478,403
Cologne (Köln), Germany
(1,830,000) 964,311
Colombo, Sri Lanka
(2,050,000) 612,000
Columbus, Ohio, U.S.
(1,243,700) 711,470
Conakry, Guinea 950,000
Copenhagen (København),
Denmark (2,030,000) 499,148
Cordoba, Argentina
(1,260,000) 1,179,067
Curitiba, Brazil
(2,595,000) 1,586,848
Dakar, Senegal 1,490,450
Dalian (Lüda), China 2,400,000
Dallas, Texas, U.S.
(4,809,300) 1,188,580
Damascus (Dimashq),
Syria (2,230,000) 1,549,932
Dar es Salaam, Tanzania 1,096,000
Delhi, India (12,791,458) 9,817,439
Denver, Colorado, U.S.
(2,148,100) 554,636
Detroit, Michigan, U.S.
(4,668,000) 951,270
Dhaka (Dacca),
Bangladesh (6,537,308) 3,637,892
Dnipropetrovs'k, Ukraine
(1,590,000) 1,147,000
Donets'k, Ukraine
(2,090,000) 1,088,000
Dresden, Germany
(860,000) 459,222
Dublin (Baile Átha Cliath),
Ireland (1,175,000) 481,854
Durban, South Africa
(1,740,000) 715,669
Düsseldorf, Germany
(1,200,000) 529,062
Edinburgh, Scotland,
U.K. (640,000) 401,910
Essen, Germany
(5,040,000) 608,732
Faisalabad, Pakistan 1,104,209
Florence (Firenze), Italy
(640,000) 381,762
Fortaleza, Brazil
(2,780,000) 788,956
Frankfurt am Main,
Germany (1,960,000) 643,469
Fukuoka, Japan
(2,000,000) 1,284,795
Gdańsk (Danzig), Poland
(885,000) 457,937
Geneva (Génève),
Switzerland (470,000) 171,042
Genoa (Genova), Italy
(800,000) 655,704
Glasgow, Scotland, U.K.
(1,870,000) 662,954
Goiânia, Brazil 1,075,761
Guadalajara, Mexico
(3,669,021) 1,646,183
Guangzhou (Canton),
China 3,750,000
Guatemala, Guatemala
(1,500,000) 823,301
Guayaquil, Ecuador 1,508,444
Ḥalab, Syria (1,640,000) 1,591,400
Ḣamburg, Germany
(2,460,000) 1,704,731
Hannover, Germany
(1,015,000) 520,670
Hanoi, Vietnam
(1,275,000) 905,939
Harare, Zimbabwe
(1,470,000) 1,189,103
Harbin, China 3,120,000
Havana (La Habana),
Cuba (2,285,000) 2,189,716
Helsinki, Finland
(1,075,000) 512,686
Hiroshima, Japan
(1,600,000) 1,108,888
Ho Chi Minh City (Saigon),
Vietnam (3,300,000) 2,796,229
Hong Kong (Xianggang),
China (4,770,000) 1,250,993
Honolulu, Hawaii, U.S.
(881,500) 371,657
Houston, Texas, U.S.
(4,178,400) 1,953,631
Hyderābād, India
(5,533,640) 3,449,878
Ibadan, Nigeria 1,144,000
Indianapolis, Indiana,
U.S. (1,397,100) 781,870

İstanbul, Turkey
(7,550,000) 6,620,241
İzmir, Turkey (1,900,000) 1,757,414
Jakarta, Indonesia
(10,200,000) 8,227,746
Jerusalem, Israel
(685,000) 633,700
Jiddah, Saudi Arabia 1,300,000
Jinan, China 2,150,000
Johannesburg, South
Africa (4,000,000) 712,507
Kābol, Afghanistan 1,424,400
Kampala, Uganda 773,463
Kānpur, India (2,690,486) 2,540,069
Kansas City, Missouri,
U.S. (1,584,200) 441,545
Kaohsiung, Taiwan
(1,900,000) 1,401,239
Karāchi, Pakistan
(5,300,000) 4,901,627
Katowice, Poland
(2,755,000) 343,158
Kazan', Russia
(1,175,000) 1,100,800
Kharkiv, Ukraine
(1,950,000) 1,555,000
Khartoum (Al Kharṭūm),
Sudan (1,450,000) 473,597
Kiev (Kyïv), Ukraine
(3,250,000) 2,630,000
Kingston, Jamaica
(830,000) 516,500
Kinshasa, Dem. Rep.
of the Congo 3,000,000
Kitakyūshū, Japan
(1,550,000) 1,019,598
Kōbe, Japan (*Ōsaka) 1,423,792
Kolkata (Calcutta), India
(13,216,546) 4,580,544
Kuala Lumpur, Malaysia
(2,500,000) 1,297,526
Kunming, China 1,500,000
Kuwait (Al Kuwayt),
Kuwait (1,126,000) 28,859
Kyōto, Japan (*Ōsaka) 1,463,822
Lagos, Nigeria
(3,800,000) 1,213,000
Lahore, Pakistan
(3,025,000) 2,707,215
La Paz, Bolivia
(1,487,854) 792,611
Leeds, England, U.K.
(1,530,000) 424,194
Liège, Belgium (747,000) 194,596
Lille, France (1,143,125) 184,657
Lima, Peru (4,608,010) 371,122
Lisbon (Lisboa), Portugal
(2,350,000) 663,394
Liverpool, England, U.K.
(1,515,000) 481,786
London, England, U.K.
(12,000,000) 7,650,944
Los Angeles, California,
U.S. (13,144,700) 3,694,820
Luanda, Angola 1,459,900
Lucknow, India
(2,266,933) 2,207,340
Lusaka, Zambia 982,362
Lyon, France (1,648,216) 445,452
Madrid, Spain
(4,690,000) 2,882,860
Managua, Nicaragua 864,201
Manaus, Brazil 1,394,724
Manchester, England, U.K.
(2,760,000) 402,889
Manila, Philippines
(11,200,000) 1,654,761
Mannheim, Germany
(1,525,000) 310,475
Maputo, Mozambique 966,837
Maracaibo, Venezuela 1,249,670
Marseille, France
(1,516,340) 798,430
Mashhad, Iran 1,887,405
Mecca (Makkah),
Saudi Arabia 550,000
Medan, Indonesia 1,730,052
Medellín, Colombia
(2,290,000) 1,551,160
Melbourne, Australia
(3,040,000) 48,560
Memphis, Tennessee,
U.S. (1,080,900) 650,100
Mexico City, Mexico
(17,786,983) 8,605,539
Miami, Florida, U.S.
(5,060,000) 362,470
Milan (Milano), Italy
(3,790,000) 1,305,591
Milwaukee, Wisconsin,
U.S. (1,619,000) 596,974
Minneapolis, Minnesota,
U.S. (2,726,600) 382,618
Minsk, Belarus
(1,722,000) 1,661,000
Mogadishu, Somalia 600,000

Monterrey, Mexico
(3,236,604) 1,110,909
Montevideo, Uruguay
(1,650,000) 1,303,182
Montréal, Canada
(3,326,510) 1,016,376
Moscow (Moskva),
Russia (12,850,000) 8,389,700
Mumbai (Bombay),
India (16,368,084) 11,914,398
Munich (München),
Germany (1,930,000) 1,205,923
Nagoya, Japan
(5,250,000) 2,152,184
Nāgpur, India (2,122,965) 2,051,320
Nairobi, Kenya 2,143,254
Nanjing, China 2,490,000
Naples (Napoli), Italy
(3,150,000) 1,046,987
Nashville, Tennessee,
U.S. (926,600) 545,524
New Delhi, India
(*Delhi) 294,783
New Orleans, Louisiana,
U.S. (1,247,700) 484,674
New York, New York,
U.S. (19,549,900) 8,008,278
Nizhniy Novgorod, Russia
(1,950,000) 1,364,900
Novosibirsk, Russia
(1,505,000) 1,402,400
Nürnberg, Germany
(1,065,000) 489,758
Odesa, Ukraine
(1,150,000) 1,046,000
Oklahoma City, Oklahoma,
U.S. (986,900) 506,132
Omsk, Russia (1,190,000) 1,157,600
Ōsaka, Japan (17,050,000) 2,602,421
Oslo, Norway (773,498) 504,040
Ottawa, Canada (1,010,498) 323,340
Panamá, Panama (995,000) 415,964
Paris, France (11,174,743) 2,125,246
Perm', Russia (1,110,000) 1,017,100
Perth, Australia (1,244,320) 10,195
Philadelphia, Pennsylvania,
U.S. (5,843,000) 1,517,550
**Phnum Pénh (Phnom
Penh),** Cambodia 570,155
Phoenix, Arizona,
U.S. (3,198,100) 1,321,045
Pittsburgh, Pennsylvania,
U.S. (2,002,700) 334,563
Poona (Pune), India
(3,755,525) 2,540,069
Port-au-Prince, Haiti
(1,425,594) 846,247
Portland, Oregon,
U.S. (1,810,200) 529,121
Porto Alegre, Brazil
(3,375,000) 1,304,998
Prague (Praha), Czech
Republic (1,328,000) 1,214,174
Pretoria, South Africa
(1,100,000) 525,583
Providence, Rhode Island,
U.S. (1,030,400) 173,618
Puebla, Mexico
(2,343,073) 1,271,673
Pusan, South Korea
(3,800,000) 3,797,566
P'yŏngyang, North Korea 2,355,000
Qingdao, China 2,300,000
Québec, Canada (671,889) 167,264
Quezon City, Philippines
(*Manila) 1,989,419
Quito, Ecuador
(1,300,000) 1,100,847
Rabat, Morocco (1,200,000) 717,000
Recife, Brazil (3,160,000) 1,421,993
Rīga, Latvia (1,000,000) 874,200
Rio de Janerio, Brazil
(10,465,000) 5,851,914
Riyadh, Saudi Arabia 1,250,000
Rome (Roma), Italy
(3,235,000) 2,649,765
Rosario, Argentina
(1,190,000) 894,645
Rostov-na-Donu, Russia
(1,160,000) 1,017,300
Rotterdam, Netherlands
(1,089,979) 539,000
St. Louis, Missouri,
U.S. (2,345,800) 348,189
St. Petersburg (Leningrad),
Russia (6,000,000) 4,728,200
Salt Lake City, Utah,
U.S. (1,018,500) 181,743
Salvador, Brazil
(2,855,000) 2,439,823
Samara, Russia
(1,450,000) 1,168,000
San Antonio, Texas, U.S.
(1,432,100) 1,144,646
San Diego, California, U.S.
(2,775,400) 1,223,400

San Francisco, California,
U.S. (6,071,300) 776,733
San José, Costa Rica
(996,194) 309,672
San Juan, Puerto Rico
(1,967,627) 421,958
San Salvador, El Salvador
(1,250,000) 415,346
Santiago, Chile
(4,740,000) 4,295,593
Santo Domingo, Dominican
Rep. 1,609,966
Santos, Brazil 415,543
São Paulo, Brazil
(17,380,000) 9,713,692
Sapporo, Japan
(2,000,000) 1,757,025
Sarajevo, Bosnia and
Herzegovina 367,703
Saratov, Russia (1,135,000) 881,000
Seattle, Washington, U.S.
(3,095,700) 563,662
Seoul (Sŏul), South Korea
(15,850,000) 10,627,790
Shanghai, China
(11,010,000) 8,930,000
Shenyang (Mukden),
China 4,050,000
Singapore, Singapore
(4,400,000) 4,017,700
Skopje, Macedonia 440,577
Sofia (Sofiya), Bulgaria
(1,280,000) 1,190,126
Stockholm, Sweden
(1,491,726) 674,452
Stuttgart, Germany
(2,020,000) 585,274
Surabaya, Indonesia 2,473,272
Sydney, Australia
(3,741,290) 11,115
Taegu, South Korea 2,228,834
T'aipei, Taiwan
(6,200,000) 2,706,453
Taiyuan, China 1,720,000
Tampa, Florida, U.S.
(1,005,500) 303,447
Tashkent, Uzbekistan
(2,325,000) 2,113,300
Tbilisi, Georgia
(1,460,000) 1,279,000
Tegucigalpa, Honduras 576,661
Tehrān, Iran (8,800,000) 6,758,845
Tel Aviv-Yafo, Israel
(1,890,000) 348,100
The Hague ('s-Gravenhage),
Netherlands (701,211) 440,743
Tianjin (Tientsin), China 5,000,000
Tiranë, Albania 243,000
Tōkyō, Japan
(30,300,000) 7,967,614
Toronto, Canada
(4,263,757) 2,385,421
Tripoli (Tarābulus), Libya
(960,000) 591,062
Tunis, Tunisia (1,300,000) 674,142
Turin (Torino), Italy
(1,550,000) 921,485
Ufa, Russia (1,110,000) 1,088,900
Ulan Bator, Mongolia 649,797
Valencia, Spain (1,340,000) 739,014
Vancouver, Canada
(1,831,665) 514,008
Venice (Venezia), Italy
(420,000) 297,743
Vienna (Wien), Austria
(1,950,000) 1,609,631
Vilnius, Lithuania 578,639
Vladivostok, Russia 613,100
Volgograd (Stalingrad),
Russia (1,358,000) 1,000,000
Warsaw (Warszawa), Poland
(2,300,000) 1,615,369
Washington, D.C., U.S.
(4,657,700) 572,059
Wellington, New Zealand
(375,000) 150,301
Winnipeg, Canada
(667,209) 618,477
Wuhan, China 3,870,000
Xi'an, China 2,410,000
Xinjiulong (New Kowloon),
China (*Hong Kong) 1,526,910
Yangon (Rangoon),
Myanmar (2,800,000) 2,705,039
Yekaterinburg, Russia
(1,530,000) 1,272,900
Yerevan, Armenia
(1,315,000) 1,199,000
Yokohama, Japan
(*Tōkyō) 3,307,136
Zagreb, Croatia 867,865
Zurich, Switzerland
(870,000) 365,043

World Facts and Comparisons

General Information

Equatorial diameter of the earth, 7,926.38 miles (12,756.27 km.).

Polar diameter of the earth, 7,899.80 miles (12,713.50 km.).

Mean diameter of the earth, 7,917.52 miles (12,742.01 km.).

Equatorial circumference of the earth, 24,901.46 miles (40,075.02 km.).

Polar circumference of the earth, 24,855.34 miles (40,000.79 km.).

Mean distance from the earth to the sun, 93,020,000 miles (149,700,000 km.).

Mean distance from the earth to the moon, 238,857 miles (384,403 km.).

Total area of the earth, 197,000,000 sq. miles (510,100,000 sq. km.).

Highest elevation on the earth's surface, Mt. Everest, Asia, 29,028 ft. (8,848 m.).

Lowest elevation on the earth's land surface, shores of the Dead Sea, Asia, 1,339 ft. (408 m.) below sea level.

Greatest known depth of the ocean, southwest of Guam, Pacific Ocean, 35,810 ft. (10,915 m.).

Total land area of the earth (incl. inland water and Antarctica), 57,900,000 sq. miles (150,100,000 sq. km.).

Area of Africa, 11,700,000 sq. miles (30,300,000 sq. km.).

Area of Antarctica, 5,400,000 sq. miles (14,000,000 sq. km.).

Area of Asia, 17,300,000 sq. miles (44,900,000 sq. km.).

Area of Europe, 3,800,000 sq. miles (9,900,000 sq. km.).

Area of North America, 9,500,000 sq. miles (24,700,000 sq. km.).

Area of Oceania (incl. Australia) 3,300,000 sq. miles (8,500,000 sq. km.).

Area of South America, 6,900,000 sq. miles (17,800,000 sq. km.).

Population of the earth (est. 1/1/04), 6,339,505,000.

Principal Islands and Their Areas

ISLAND	Area (Sq. Mi.)	(Sq. Km)
Baffin I., Canada	195,928	507,451
Banks I., Canada	27,038	70,028
Borneo (Kalimantan), Asia	287,299	744,100
Bougainville, Papua New Guinea	3,591	9,300
Cape Breton I., Canada	3,981	10,311
Celebes (Sulawesi), Indonesia	73,057	189,216
Corsica, France	3,367	8,720
Crete, Greece	3,189	8,259
Cuba, N. America	42,760	110,800
Cyprus, Asia	3,572	9,251
Devon I., Canada	21,331	55,247
Ellesmere I., Canada	75,767	196,236
Great Britain, U.K.	88,795	229,978
Greenland, N. America	840,004	2,175,600
Hainan Dao, China	13,127	34,000
Hawaii, U.S.	4,021	10,414
Hispaniola, N. America	29,421	76,200
Hokkaidō, Japan	32,245	83,515
Honshū, Japan	89,176	239,966
Iceland, Europe	39,769	103,000
Ireland, Europe	32,587	84,400
Jamaica, N. America	4,247	11,000
Java (Jawa), Indonesia	51,038	132,187
Kodiak I., U.S.	3,670	9,505
Kyūshū, Japan	17,129	44,363
Long Island, U.S.	1,377	3,566
Luzon, Philippines	40,420	104,688
Madagascar, Africa	226,642	587,000
Melville I., Canada	16,274	42,149
Mindanao, Philippines	36,537	94,630
New Britain, Papua New Guinea	14,093	36,500
New Caledonia, Oceania	6,252	16,192
Newfoundland, Canada	42,031	108,860
New Guinea, Asia-Oceania	308,882	800,000
North I., New Zealand	44,333	114,821
Novaya Zemlya, Russia	31,892	82,600
Prince of Wales I., Canada	12,872	33,339
Puerto Rico, N. America	3,514	9,104
Sakhalin, Russia	29,498	76,400
Sardinia, Italy	9,301	24,090
Sicily, Italy	9,926	25,709
South I., New Zealand	57,708	149,463
Southampton I., Canada	15,913	41,214
Spitsbergen, Norway	15,260	39,523
Sri Lanka, Asia	24,942	64,600
Sumatra (Sumatera), Indonesia	182,860	473,606
Taiwan, Asia	13,900	36,000
Tasmania, Australia	26,178	67,800
Tierra del Fuego, S. America	18,600	48,174
Timor, Asia	5,743	14,874
Vancouver I., Canada	12,079	31,285
Victoria I., Canada	83,897	217,291

Principal Lakes, Oceans, Seas and Their Areas

LAKE Country	Area (Sq. Mi.)	(Sq. Km.)
Arabian Sea	1,492,000	3,863,000
Aral Sea, Kazakhstan-Uzbekistan	14,900	38,600
Arctic Ocean	5,400,000	14,000,000
Athabasca, L., Canada	3,064	7,935
Atlantic Ocean	29,600,000	76,800,000
Baikal, L. (Ozero Baykal), Russia	12,162	31,500
Balkash, L., Kazakhstan	7,066	18,301
Baltic Sea, Europe	163,000	422,000
Bering Sea, Asia-N.A.	876,000	2,270,000
Black Sea, Europe-Asia	178,000	461,000
Caribbean Sea, N.A.-S.A.	1,063,000	2,754,000
Caspian Sea, Asia-Europe	143,200	371,000
Chad, L., Cameroon-Chad-Nigeria	6,300	16,300
Erie, L., Canada-U.S.	9,910	25,667
Eyre, L., Australia	3,700	9,600
Great Bear Lake, Canada	12,095	31,326
Great Salt Lake, U.S.	1,680	4,351
Great Slave Lake, Canada	11,030	28,568
Hudson Bay, Canada	475,000	1,230,000
Huron, L., Canada-U.S.	23,000	59,600
Indian Ocean	26,500,000	68,600,000
Japan, Sea of, Asia	389,000	1,008,000
Ladozhskoye Ozero (L. Ladoga), Russia	6,800	17,700
Manitoba, L., Canada	1,785	4,624
Mediterranean Sea, Europe-Africa-Asia	967,000	2,505,000
Mexico, Gulf of, N. America	596,000	1,544,000
Michigan, L., U.S.	22,300	57,800
Nicaragua, Lago de, Nicaragua	3,150	8,158
North Sea, Europe	222,000	575,000
Nyasa, L., Malawi-Mozambique-Tanzania	11,150	28,878
Onezhskoye Ozero (L. Onega), Russia	3,753	9,720
Ontario, L., Canada-U.S.	7,540	19,529
Pacific Ocean	60,100,000	155,600,000
Red Sea, Africa-Asia	169,000	438,000
Rudolf, L., Ethiopia-Kenya	2,473	6,405
Southern Ocean	7,800,000	20,300,00
Superior, L., Canada-U.S.	31,700	82,100
Tanganyika, L., Africa	12,350	31,986
Titicaca, Lago, Bolivia-Peru	3,200	8,300
Torrens, L., Australia	2,278	5,900
Victoria, L., Kenya-Tanzania-Uganda	26,820	69,464
Winnipeg, L., Canada	9,416	24,387
Winnipegosis, L., Canada	2,075	5,374
Yellow Sea, China-Korea	480,000	1,240,000

Principal Mountains and Their Heights

MOUNTAIN Country	Elev. (Ft.)	(M.)
Aconcagua, Cerro, Argentina	22,831	6,959
Ağrı Dağı, Turkey	16,854	5,137
Annapurna, Nepal	26,545	8,091
Aoraki, New Zealand	12,316	3,754
Bia, Phou, Laos	9,252	2,820
Blanc, Mont (Monte Bianco), France-Italy	15,771	4,807
Bolívar, Pico, Venezuela	16,427	5,007
Borah Pk., Idaho, U.S.	12,662	3,859
Boundary Pk., Nevada, U.S.	13,143	4,006
Cameroon Mtn., Cameroon	13,451	4,100
Carrauntoohil, Ireland	3,406	1,038
Chaltel, Cerro (Monte Fitzroy), Argentina-Chile	10,958	3,340
Chimborazo, Ecuador	20,702	6,310
Chirripó, Cerro, Costa Rica	12,530	3,819
Cristóbal Colón, Pico, Colombia	18,947	5,775
Damāvand, Qolleh-ye, Iran	18,386	5,604
Duarte, Pico, Dominican Rep.	10,417	3,175
Dufourspitze (Monte Rosa), Italy-Switzerland	15,203	4,634
Elbert, Mt., Colorado, U.S.	14,433	4,399
El'brus, Gora, Russia	18,510	5,642
Etna, Mt., Italy	10,902	3,323
Everest, Mt., China-Nepal	29,028	8,848
Fairweather, Mt., Alaska-Canada	15,300	4,663
Fuji, Mt., Japan	12,388	3,776
Galdhøpiggen, Norway	8,100	2,469
Gannett Pk., Wyoming, U.S.	13,804	4,207
Gerlachovský Stit, Slovakia	8,711	2,655
Giluwe, Mt., Papua New Guinea	14,331	4,368
Grand Teton, Wyoming, U.S.	13,770	4,197
Grossglockner, Austria	12,457	3,797
Haleakalā Crater, Hawaii, U.S.	10,032	3,058
Hood, Mt., Oregon, U.S.	11,239	3,426
Huascarán, Nevado, Peru	22,133	6,746
Illampu, Nevado, Bolivia	21,066	6,421
Illimani, Nevado de, Bolivia	21,184	6,457
Ismail Samani, pik, Tajikistan	24,590	7,495
Iztaccíhuatl, Mexico	17,159	5,230
Jaya, Puncak, Indonesia	16,503	5,030
Jungfrau, Switzerland	13,642	4,158
K2 (Godwin Austen), China-Pakistan	28,250	8,611
Kānchenjunga, India-Nepal	28,208	8,598
Kātrīnā, Jabal, Egypt	8,668	2,642
Kebnekaise, Sweden	6,926	2,111
Kilimanjaro, Tanzania	19,340	5,895
Kinabalu, Gunong, Malaysia	13,455	4,101
Kirinyaga (Mt. Kenya), Kenya	17,058	5,199
Klyuchevskaya Sopka, Vulkan, Russia	15,584	4,750
Kosciuszko, Mt., Australia	7,313	2,229
Koussi, Emi, Chad	11,204	3,415
Kula Kangri, Bhutan	24,784	7,554
Lassen Pk., California, U.S.	10,457	3,187
Llullaillaco, Volcán, Argentina-Chile	22,110	6,739
Logan, Mt., Canada	19,551	5,959
Margherita Peak, D.R.C. of the Congo-Uganda	16,763	5,109
Markham, Mt., Antarctica	14,049	4,282
Matterhorn, Italy-Switzerland	14,692	4,478
Mauna Loa, Hawaii, U.S.	13,677	4,169
Mayon Volcano, Philippines	8,077	2,462
McKinley, Mt., Alaska, U.S.	20,320	6,194
Mitchell, Mt., North Carolina, U.S.	6,684	2,037
Mulhacén, Spain (continental)	11,424	3,482
Musala, Bulgaria	9,596	2,925
Nabî Shu'ayb, Jabal an-, Yemen	12,008	3,660
Nanda Devi, India	25,645	7,817
Nānga Parbat, Pakistan	26,660	8,126
Narodnaya, Gora, Russia	6,214	1,894
Nevis, Ben, United Kingdom	4,406	1,343
Ojos del Salado, Nevado, Argentina-Chile	22,615	6,893
Ólimbos, Greece	9,570	2,917
Olympus, Mt., Washington, U.S.	7,969	2,429
Orizaba, Pico de, Mexico	18,406	5,610
Paektu San, North Korea-China	9,003	2,744
Paricutín, Mexico	9,186	2,800
Pelée, Montagne, Martinique	4,583	1,397
Pikes Pk., Colorado, U.S.	14,110	4,301
Pobedy, pik, China-Kyrgyzstan	24,406	7,439
Popocatépetl, Volcán, Mexico	17,930	5,465
Rainier, Mt., Washington, U.S.	14,411	4,392
Ras Dashen Terara, Ethiopia	15,158	4,620
Robson, Mt., Canada	12,972	3,954
Roraima, Mt., Brazil-Guyana-Venezuela	9,432	2,875
Ruapehu, Mt., New Zealand	9,177	2,797
Sajama, Nevado, Bolivia	21,463	6,542
Shasta, Mt., California, U.S.	14,162	4,317
Tahat, Algeria	9,541	2,908
Tajumulco, Volcán, Guatemala	13,845	4,220
Tirich Mīr, Pakistan	25,230	7,690
Toubkal, Jebel, Morocco	13,665	4,165
Turquino, Pico, Cuba	6,470	1,972
Uluru (Ayers Rock), Australia	2,831	863
Vesuvius, Italy	4,203	1,281
Victoria, Mt., Papua New Guinea	13,238	4,035
Vinson Massif, Antarctica	16,066	4,897
Washington, Mt., New Hampshire, U.S.	6,288	1,917
Whitney, Mt., California, U.S.	14,494	4,418
Wilhelm, Mt., Papua New Guinea	14,793	4,509
Wrangell, Mt., Alaska, U.S.	14,163	4,317
Yü Shan, Taiwan	13,	
Zugspitze, Austria-Germany	9,7	

Principal Rivers and Their Lengths

RIVER Continent	Length (Mi.)	
Aldan, Asia	1,412	
Amazonas-Ucayali, S. America	3,900	
Amu Darya, Asia	1,578	
Amur, Asia	2,744	
Araguaia, S. America	1,367	
Arkansas, N. America	1,459	2
Athabasca, N. America	765	1,
Ayeyarwady, Asia	1,300	2,0
Brahmaputra, Asia	1,770	2,84
Canadian, N. America	906	1,45
Churchill, N. America	1,000	1,60
Colorado, N. America (U.S.-Mexico)	1,450	2,334
Columbia, N. America	1,243	2,000
Congo (Zaïre), Africa	2,880	4,635
Danube, Europe	1,776	2,858
Darling, Australia	864	1,390
Dnieper, Europe	1,367	2,200
Dniester, Europe	840	1,352
Don, Europe	1,162	1,870
Elbe, Europe	720	1,159
Euphrates, Asia	1,510	2,430
Fraser, N. America	851	1,370
Ganges, Asia	1,560	2,511
Godāvari, Asia	930	1,497
Green, N. America	730	1,175
Huang (Yellow), Asia	3,395	5,464
Indus, Asia	1,800	2,897
Kama, Europe	1,122	1,805
Kasai, Africa	1,338	2,153
Kolyma, Asia	1,323	2,129
Lena, Asia	2,734	4,400
Limpopo, Africa	1,100	1,770
Mackenzie, N. America	2,635	4,241
Madeira, S. America	2,013	3,240
Marañón, S. America	1,000	1,600
Mekong, Asia	2,600	4,18
Mississippi, N. America	2,348	3,77
Missouri, N. America	2,315	3,72
Murray, Australia	1,566	2,52
Negro, S. America	1,305	2,10
Niger, Africa	2,600	4,18
Nile, Africa	4,145	6,67
North Platte, N. America	618	99
Ob'-Irtysh, Asia	3,362	5,41
Ohio, N. America	981	1,57
Orange, Africa	1,300	2,0
Orinoco, S. America	1,600	2,57
Ottawa, N. America	790	1,2
Paraguay, S. America	1,610	
Paraná, S. America	2,796	
Peace, N. America	1,195	
Pechora, Europe	1,124	
Pecos, N. America	735	1,
Pilcomayo, S. America	1,550	2,
Plata-Paraná, S. America	3,030	4,8
Purús, S. America	1,860	2,9
Red, N. America	1,270	2,04
Rhine, Europe	820	1,320
Rio Grande, N. America	1,885	3,034
St. Lawrence, N. America	800	1,287
Salween (Nu), Asia	1,750	2,816
São Francisco, S. America	1,988	3,199
Saskatchewan-Bow, N. America	1,205	1,939
Snake, N. America	1,038	1,670
Syr Darya, Asia	1,370	2,205
Tarim, Asia	1,328	2,137
Tigris, Asia	1,180	1,899
Tocantins, S. America	1,640	2,639
Ucayali, S. America	1,220	1,963
Ural, Asia	1,509	2,428
Uruguay, S. America	1,025	1,650
Verkhnyaya Tunguska (Angara), Asia	1,105	1,779
Vilyuy, Asia	1,647	2,650
Volga, Asia	2,194	3,531
Xingu, S. America	1,230	1,979
Yangtze (Chang), Asia	3,915	6,300
Yenisey, Asia	2,543	4,092
Yukon, N. America	1,979	3,185
Zambezi, Africa	1,700	2,736